YOUR WORLD

CHANGING COMMUNITIES FOR GOOD

Debra Green OBE

RIVER
PUBLISHING

River Publishing & Media Ltd
Barham Court
Teston
Maidstone
Kent
ME18 5BZ
United Kingdom

info@river-publishing.co.uk

ISBN 978-1-908393-40-1
Printed by Bell and Bain, Glasgow
Cover design by www.SpiffingCovers.com

CONTENTS

DEDICATION

This book is dedicated to:
Josiah, Mimi-Raie, Liberty, and Noah

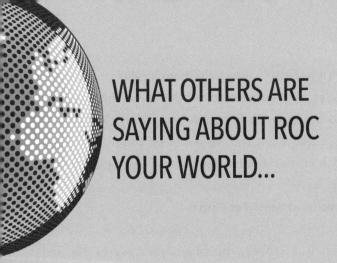

WHAT OTHERS ARE SAYING ABOUT ROC YOUR WORLD...

"Debra has followed the leadings of God and has found that a model of multi-agency partnership, mixed with meeting the most pressing local needs, mixed with prayer and faith really works."

Ness Wilson
Senior Leader, Open Heaven Church, Loughborough

"I like ROC's approach to improving community life and am glad to see projects already taking root in Scotland."

Sally Magnusson
Broadcaster

"Finally the Church is waking up to the enormous opportunities to demonstrate the Gospel to our communities. Redeeming Our Communities is leading the charge."

Alan McWilliam
Leader, Whiteinch Church of Scotland and Clan Gathering

"Bursting with hope this wonderful book inspires, challenges and encourages all at the same time! Our communities can be restored and this amazing book will be a catalyst for greater change. Buy it and live it and we will begin to see our nation transformed in the name of Jesus, one community at a time."

Gavin Calver

National Director of Youth For Christ

"Debra Green is a pioneer, pressing into areas of life and ministry where the Church is called to be. This book demands a response. God has called us to partner with him in his mission. Debra paints a picture of the difference we can make if we love as Christ's disciples in the world around us. Don't just read this book, live it!"

Malcolm Duncan

Leader, Goldhill Baptist Church; Chair, Spring Harvest Planning Group

"If you've ever wanted to change your corner of the world for good and wondered how to do it, here is your essential guide. Few people have the know-how and experience to write it, but as you read Debra's inspirational stories of God's redeeming love and power, I defy you not to get up from your armchair and go out with a new passion and excitement to follow the call of Jesus wherever he takes you."

Michele Guinness

Author and speaker

"Over the last 20 years Debra Green has learnt vital lessons in reaching out to communities, combining prayer and relationship

building with Holy Spirit inspired action and ROC has emerged as a gift to the body of Christ in the UK. With 50 projects already up and running, thousands are being helped every week. This is the Church at work, combining the good news of the Gospel with very practical demonstrations of God's love in action. This book will inspire and equip us to better serve Jesus in his mission to the world."

Steve Clifford
General Director, Evangelical Alliance

"Sometimes change needs a helping hand – especially change for the better, and that is exactly what ROC is doing by pulling together all sectors of the community for the benefit of the community. ROC is growing and it's heading your way."

Midge Ure OBE
Ultravox, Co-founder Live Aid, Band Aid

"I have been really inspired by the story of Redeeming Our Communities. Debra's bold steps of faith and servant-hearted engagement are a great example to us all to step out and see hope restored to our communities."

Billy Kennedy
Senior Leader, New Community Pioneer Network

"This book will both challenge and inspire. In an age that questions whether real and lasting change is possible, read on and be encouraged!"

Matt Baggott
Chief Constable Police Service of Northern Ireland

"I rejoice in the many ways in which God has used ROC as a catalyst for community transforming ministry in so many places across our nation, and I am continually thrilled to see the impact of our own ROC Café upon young people in one of the communities served by our church. Debra Green's latest book is packed full of stories of God's work to inspire and excite you about what is possible when ordinary people partner with God to see extraordinary things come about."

Ian Parkinson

Senior Pastor All Saints Marple; Regional Director New Wine North

"ROC is about galvanising the Christian communities to get out of their churches and start engaging with their local communities and to provide help and support where it is needed most. ROC is about the Christian faith in action changing peoples' lives through deeds and not just words. As a senior police officer I see ROC as an essential part of neighbourhood policing and one that makes a real difference to local communities and peoples lives."

Paul Netherton

Assistant Chief Constable Devon and Cornwall Police

ACKNOWLEDGEMENTS

I am grateful to all the people who have contributed to this book especially to those who have written pieces, and helped with the editing. Also huge thanks to those who have supported by being involved with ROC including our staff team, regional coordinators, volunteers, project leaders, ROC Ambassadors, trustees, steering groups, partner churches, partner agencies and intercessors. And finally to the people who attend our projects, far too many to list but you are the reason we are ROC.

My thanks go to the writing, editing and media team;

Frank Green, Jabulani Mhlanga, Jerry Clifford, Nathan Stirling, Tim Pettingale, Iona and Howard Jones, Steve Holmes, Lawrence Bettany, Rebecca Green, Mandie Munro, Carol Everett, Daniel Beswick, John Berriman, Sian and Paul Hobson and Paul Hurst.

I am also grateful to: Paul Harris, Graham Simmons, Pete Dawson, Emma Gaze, Danny Wood, Paul Wilson, Roger Bartlett, Neil Collin, Ian Wills, Nicki and Pete Sims, Kevin Pickup, John McGinley, David Hind, Wendy and Mark Ashcroft, Julia Robertson, Margaret Bull, Jackie Marsh, Alan Taylor, Jenny Bailey, James Aladiran, Joshua Green, Emma Green, Matthew Green, Sarah Green, Andy Bell, Neil Wain, Faith Taylor, Annie Johnson, Paul Sohi, Keith Mitchell – Mitch, Jonny Campbell, Jennie Cloherty, Ann Russell, Matty Amey, Marian Ayres and Rob Groves.

FOREWORD

It was Albert Einstein who first described insanity as "Doing the same thing over and over again and expecting different results."

If the nation is to be changed by the love of Jesus, the Church in the UK clearly needs to be doing something different from what it has done for the last few decades. Depending on geography, anything from 85%-97% of the population of the villages, towns and cities in our nation have no meaningful, frequent connection with the Church. The impact of this increasing marginalisation is seen most starkly in our urban estates, where dysfunctional families struggle with all the issues of disempowerment and alienation caused by relational, financial and employment poverty.

There are at least three possible responses to this loss of Christian influence in the nation. One is for the Church to retreat even further into isolation and exclusivism, continuing to practise its worship, ministry and mission as it has for decades. The consequence? A slow but certain death. A second response is for the Church to try to turn up the volume of its acerbic proclamation of the uniqueness of Jesus and its criticism of alternative lifestyles and moral philosophies. I believe the consequence will be a further distancing of most from the love of Jesus. Very few respond to this type of judgemental approach.

In this book Debra Green not only talks about the possibility of a better response, but presents evidence of the fruitfulness of this approach. The work of ROC has expanded rapidly over the last decade and is based on a number of key principles, four of which I will draw attention to here.

First is the belief that God still has a heart for his broken world and is longing to bring his help and healing to the broken and needy today, in the same way he demonstrated through the incarnation and ministry of our Lord Jesus Christ. The ministry of the Church, the visible body of Christ in our generation, needs to be as much about the goodness, generosity and grace of God now as it was then. The story of ROC is the story of "The kindness of God [that] leads to repentance" (Romans 2.4). The demonstration of the Gospel of the Kingdom must go alongside the proclamation of the uniqueness of the King. It is the bridge of kindness that ROC builds that enables many to walk, or even run, into the Kingdom who may never have responded to mere proclamation.

Second is the belief that God has planted sufficient resources in every community to be the means of bringing change and a different future to that community. Some of those resources are within the Church and some are within the hearts and lives of other people of goodwill in the community. When those resources are placed in the hands of God (from whom they originated) then he multiplies them in such a way that they bring hope to thousands. The story of the feeding of the five thousand from one boy's packed lunch can be repeated in our communities when we offer back to God who we are and what we have (however little that may seem).

Third is a belief in partnership. Instead of engaging in "ministry" to a community, ROC has learnt how to listen to the community, engage with others who have a similar longing for change, and then work together for the transformation wanted by all. The way in which ROC centres have brought together numbers of churches and statutory services is powerful and persuasive of the greater efficacy of this approach over and against the commonly held belief and practice of one (normally my) church being either uniquely or best qualified to satisfy every need in the community. The extension of the Kingdom of God has always been dependent on there being more workers in the harvest-field – that's why Jesus taught us to pray for them (Matthew 9.38). The approach of ROC has found a radical way of addressing this critical issue.

The fourth principle I point to here is faith exercised through prayer. At every stage of the journey Debra has gone way beyond what "common sense" might have indicated was possible. She has caught a glimpse of what might be possible, and then prayed that dream or vision into visible reality. Sometimes others have immediately joined her, but sometimes she has pioneered for some time on her own before others have caught up with and then journeyed with her. Her faith in her God has been infectious and whole communities have now benefitted as a result. The assertion that "real faith can move mountains" (Matthew 21.21) has become true as mountains of impossible things have been moved and a highway for God's grace has been built.

For those who believe the Church is meant to be a faithful remnant living within well defended walls of exclusivity the story of ROC is a threat. For those who believe the Church is meant to be the joyful, hopeful people of God sent by our Lord to transform every nook, cranny and community of our nation this book offers a proven way of becoming what we long to be. Following Jesus is meant to be the greatest adventure on earth. This book offers us all an invitation, once again, to join that adventure with fresh hope, faith and love.

John Coles
National Director, New Wine

PREFACE

The aim of this book is to inspire, empower and equip readers to engage in community transformation. To see *your* community changed for good.

Through this book I hope you will learn two things: firstly, that the principles contained herein *are* transferable to your situation, your community, and will answer the needs you see. Secondly, that *you* are capable of bringing the change; capable, with God's help, of so much more than you ever imagined. In time, I want you to be able to tell your story of transformation, which you can do via the **www.rocyourworld.org** blog.

The spiritual truths and principles in this book were learned over many years, from launching the Redeeming Our Communities (ROC) initiative in Manchester and seeing it grow and spread far and wide. Not everyone will have heard of ROC, so by way of introduction here is a brief history to set the stage for the remainder of the book.

THE ROC STORY

In 1993 I initiated a city-wide, inter-church Prayer Network, which focused on different themes to pray for our city of Manchester. By 1998 we held a special meeting to pray for members of Greater Manchester Police. In conjunction with this meeting we placed "Thank You" posters in every Police Station across the area, thanking the Police force for their efforts. The fruit of this meeting was significant. Relationships between the Church and Police across the city began to develop in an unprecedented way. Developments were such that in 2000 and 2003 Manchester was able to hold large-scale outreach festivals that brought together people across all denominations, which were backed by the Police. During these festivals prayer for the city was increased, but there was also a practical outworking of faith in some of the poorest communities. Christians came together to clean up neighbourhoods. They served the local people and were a presence for good. (The full story is told in our first book City-Changing Prayer by Debra and Frank Green, published in 2005 and recently republished).

ROC was established in 2004 as a vehicle to continue the excellent evangelistic outreach work of Festival Manchester.

I had worked full time as the Festival's partner church co-ordinator and recruited over 500 churches as active participants. One of the outstanding features of Festival Manchester was the community partnerships that were created between local churches, the Police and other agencies – all of whom shared a common goal: to see communities transformed.

My vision and passion was to enable these partnerships to continue, rather than fizzle out once the Festival finished. The Lord had clearly called me to this and I seemed to find favour with senior police officers, council leaders and other secular agencies as well as church leaders. Exciting new projects were launched, led by ROC partner churches and involving volunteers from the local community and secular groups. This helped churches to become more effective in sharing the Gospel with un-churched people and, as a result, many came to Christ. In addition, these areas of our city have seen sharp falls in crime and anti-social behaviour.

The ROC inaugural launch event in September 2004 drew thousands of Christians together from the North West to thank the Police for their work and also pledge to see violent crime reduced in the region over the next 12 months through prayer and action. The pledge was met: 6 months after that meeting the Metro newspaper reported that violent crime in the region had fallen by 11.5%, bucking national trends.

Churches across the UK heard about ROC's unique approach to community transformation and, during the last ten years, ROC has been invited to help establish many new projects in almost every corner of the UK and Northern Ireland – especially in some of the most deprived areas.

People from around the country were beginning to grasp the vision of ROC and demand was such that a National Launch was held in 2006 at the NEC Arena. Over 7,000 people attended, including VIP guests from the Police, Fire and Rescue Service, local government and Parliament. After the National Launch the initiative grew further, with ROC Ambassadors being established in regions throughout the UK. We began to hear stories of community transformation across the nation, some of which were collected together for my second book, Redeeming Our Communities: 21st Century Miracles of Social Transformation.

We also hosted several "ROC Ambassador" conferences to train and equip those who wanted to bring the ROC model to their towns and cities.

In June 2008, we held another city-wide, large-scale event to tackle the issue of gang culture and gun and knife crime. During the event it was prayed and proclaimed that Manchester would no longer be known as "Gunchester". We were blessed to read, less than a year later, a headline in the Manchester Evening News asking, "Is this the end of Gunchester?" since there had been a 38% drop in gun-related incidents and not a single killing in 12 months.

Several representatives of police forces and nine Chief Constables from around the UK were present at the event in 2008 and began to recognise the value of working with the Church. We were approached by the Deputy Chief Constable of Merseyside Police, Bernard Lawson, to hold a launch in Liverpool. Following his appointment as Chief Constable of Greater Manchester Police, Sir Peter Fahy asked us to expand our work in Manchester. I was also invited to Aberdeen at the request of Chief Constable Colin McKerracher to speak at a Faith and Policing conference. These requests, amongst others, prompted us to consider the best strategy to take ROC forward. We felt strongly that it would be best to commit to a strategy of working closely with police forces in 10 cities or regions over the following years. It was agreed that Manchester and Merseyside would be the first of these regions. ROC has subsequently launched in other cities including Birmingham, London, Nottingham, Plymouth, Exeter, Belfast, Leicester and Glasgow. Work has also been developing in many counties and towns across England, Wales, Scotland and Northern Ireland.

ROC projects provide direct help to all age groups with a focus on youth through the ROC Café and ROC Football projects. Other projects which help the wider community include ROC Restore, a restorative justice project and ROC Care, a visiting and befriending scheme for older people.

Increasingly, statutory authorities, agencies and community groups are approaching us for the support, expertise and resources we can provide.

Today ROC has over fifty community-based projects which meet the needs of many thousands of people every week and address a variety of social issues affecting young and old alike. Each project is led by a church whose mission vision combines Gospel proclamation with a practical demonstration of God's love in action. In every case the partner church is experiencing conversion growth as a direct result of reaching new people through ROC projects.

We are being sought out by Public Services and local authorities who are interested to see how they can partner with local churches to address the social needs of their communities.

You can find out more at **www.roc.uk.com**

Debra Green OBE
February 2014

A WORD ABOUT QR CODES

There are a number of extra resources accompanying this book, which can be accessed online via Quick Response (QR) Codes, which you will see appearing at relevant points throughout this book. For the uninitiated, a QR Code is a type of barcode that is readable by smart phones and other mobile devices. There are numbers of free QR code reader mobile apps on the market. Once installed on your smart phone or mobile device, scanning a QR code will direct you to the online resources, which includes film clips and audio interviews.

www.rocyourworld.org

1
MIRACLES OF MULTIPLICATION

Have you ever longed to transform the area where you live, but have no idea how to make it happen? Would you love to see relationships in your community improve and change for the better? Do you want to be part of God's miracle for your neighbourhood and beyond?

I believe you can do all of these things – and more. And all it will take is the smallest amount of faith and action on your part to set community transformation in motion. Over the last twenty years I have witnessed ordinary people, like you and me, used by God to accomplish some extraordinary things. I like to call them "miracles of multiplication" because God takes the little we have and creates something much bigger out of it. We don't need to be specially gifted or trained – just willing.

In this book I want to share with you principles learned over twenty years of seeing community transformation in action. These are not just good ideas – they work. They do transform communities – for good! Many stories from many places around the UK spring to mind, but here is a simple one to set the scene from Cobridge in Stoke-on-Trent...

CHANGE IN THE RED LIGHT DISTRICT

Iona and Howard Jones first heard about ROC – specifically the ROC Café Youth Project – at the New Wine summer festival and decided it could work for them. I'll let them tell the story:

"I guess you could say that the ROC Café in Cobridge started one afternoon as we were doing a small survey around the area, asking what the greatest local need was. Time and again came the answer, 'We need something for young people. There's nothing for them to do round here, so they hang about the streets and make trouble.'

Or perhaps it was on a cold, damp November morning when we squeezed two, somewhat sceptical, local police officers into our little car and drove up to Reddish in Stockport to investigate the ROC Café there. At the project in Reddish, a wonderfully enthusiastic Police and Community Support Officer (PCSO) talked to them in 'cop speak' about how brilliant it was. As we sat in the car later, eating fish and chips, PCSO Justine Marsh said, 'We've just got to do this in Cobridge, haven't we? I mean, we can't not.'

Cobridge is a poor area of Stoke-on-Trent, itself a poor city, with all the problems typical of impoverished urban areas around Britain. It's known as a red light area and although much of that has been officially 'cleaned up', the reputation remains. It's also an area with a high proportion of people from ethnic minorities (with many Pakistani and Bangladeshi Muslims), with the tragically common problems of outright racism, hostility, suspicion and division. Young people have low expectations of what life holds for them. The highest aspirations being, as one young lad said to us without a hint of irony, 'To get a proper job, in Argos.'

So we started. We went into schools and talked with young people to ask for their ideas. We gathered a team of local people and tried to make as many partnerships as possible. We had no resources. We hadn't got vast amounts of experience in community work, so the idea of partnership was not just an admirable value – it was an absolute necessity. We secured funding from the Police and from a Christian charity and in April 2011 we launched ROC Café Cobridge. There was an immediate, enthusiastic response from local young people. Since we opened, over three hundred young people have come through the doors of the ROC Café.

We still love doing ROC and we are seeing multiplication in so many ways. As well as the ROC Café, we've branched out into doing ROC Sport and ROC Gardens, which the young people love. Some weeks it's really hard going – we're battling attitudes and behaviour that we're not used to. But other weeks we see those little breakthroughs, where the young people make small steps of personal growth (small, but so significant!) and we go home on a high.

As with most organisations, recruiting volunteers to begin with is easier than retaining them. ROC Cobridge has been no different. Numbers will often reduce for various reasons, but the Police have remained our most loyal partners and we are so grateful for their commitment. PCSO Justine Marsh is still working with us, along with Matt Boyles and PC Mark Trafford. We've developed excellent relationships with the other volunteers and with the young people. Recently, the Police told a visitor about how the Café had made a real difference to the way in which they work. 'Before, young people would just see us as the enemy and run away. But being able to meet them socially, play games with them, help them with homework, cookery, craft and so on and know them by name has made a huge difference to the way we're able to do our community policing. By the time young people are about sixteen that window of opportunity to develop a relationship with them has gone. Being able to get alongside them while they're younger makes a real difference.'

For us, the best thing is simply the opportunity ROC Café gives us to develop relationships with the young people in our area. We've seen real improvements in our local area. To know we've played our part in that hasn't just been satisfying, it's been essential to know that we are doing the work of God in Cobridge."

The ROC Café in Cobridge has just been awarded a grant by Matthew Ellis, the Police and Crime Commissioner, that has enabled them to purchase some floodlights for their ROC Sports project. Watch the film clip using the QR code below:

I hear lots of stories like these. Iona and Howard's story is one of many encouragements that have been born out of the work of ROC. Each time I hear from the "Ionas and Howards" of our communities all over the UK, I am challenged as to how we can equip more people of goodwill to make safer, kinder communities. I want to help others make meaningful and lasting change in their towns and cities. I want to equip people to be the answer to their own prayers.

Bringing real, lasting change in your community may seem like a daunting journey for anyone who hasn't walked this kind of path before. But to paraphrase an ancient Chinese proverb: even the longest journeys start with small steps. All it takes for community change to begin is for a small group of willing people to play their part. It begins with individuals – just like you and me.

MORE ABOUT THE ROC CAFÉ MODEL

A ROC Café usually opens at least one evening a week when there is the greatest need for youth activities, traditionally on a Friday/Saturday (to help reduce anti-social behaviour). It is run by volunteers, which means it is very cost effective. Across the country youth projects are under threat of closure and this model is helping to sustain youth provision at a time when many services are closing due to cuts. Some youth clubs fail due to leaders being challenged by unruly teenagers, however the ROC Café thrives due to expert input offered by our partners including the Police and Fire and Rescue Service. Local funding is often more forthcoming for a ROC Café as we take a neutral, multi-agency approach and each agency plays a part in helping to source funds. Local grant-making trusts exist all around the country with strict guidelines that mean they can only support local projects. Many are restricted by their covenant to give only to certain types of activity and often churches or other religious bodies are excluded. ROC's neutral status overcomes this.

Many ROC Cafés have become a vital place of security and stability for the young people who attend regularly. In some cases we're told that it feels like "true family" for those youngsters from troubled backgrounds. We heard recently from Jon Kelly of Greater Manchester Police who is involved with the one of the ROC Cafés. He was chatting to a young boy whose mum works all hours to make ends meet. The boy said, "The ROC Café is the living room I don't have at home." I literally cried when I heard this. What a privilege it is to make this kind of difference in people's lives.

ROC CAFÉ AIMS

The ROC Café is designed as a safe place where positive activities and role models help young people discover purpose and value in their lives. The initial aim of the project is to reduce crime and anti-social behaviour among young people through the provision of diversionary activities, BUT with the longer term aim of helping them to develop into active citizens who are able to take responsibility for themselves, their families and communities.

A multi-agency approach is used to achieve the outcomes of the project. Within its first year of opening, the ROC Café in Reddish, Stockport, reported a 45% reduction in crime and anti-social behaviour. This trend is continuing at other locations where we have opened new ROC Cafés. A project in Winton, Salford, has just reported a 90% reduction in crime in the area where the ROC Café opened six months previously.

ROC CAFÉ OBJECTIVES:

1. Young people will have a safe, fun place to go where they can also develop life skills and play a part in improving their communities.

2. Anti-social behaviour and crime will be reduced leading to safer neighbourhoods and reduced calls on police and other agencies' time.

3. Relations between young people and authority figures will be improved which leads to better community cohesion.

4. The project will provide an opportunity for agencies and local people to work together and benefit from areas of expertise each has to offer.

THE SEED OF FAITH

One of the founding principles of ROC is that we make clear our initiatives are Christian-led, but we are open to the involvement of all people of "goodwill", regardless of whether they have a faith or not. But in practice, I have found that my work in helping to stimulate community transformation often begins in churches. This is because I have chosen to share my life with others who have deliberately chosen to follow Jesus; who believe that God brilliantly created the world we live in and has not turned His back on creation. He hasn't abandoned the human race to struggle alone with our problems – even if we have created many of them ourselves. With that in mind, I have prayed and planned with countless others for social transformation in our cities, towns and villages across the UK and beyond. Gradually, my eyes have been opened to see the many encouraging signs that God is at work, renewing and restoring our world, right in front us.

This is so encouraging. Community transformation isn't some wishful pipe dream that exists way off in the distant future. According to the teaching of Jesus in the New Testament, the Kingdom of God is advancing on the earth in real time, bringing everything into alignment with the plans and purposes of the Creator.

Jesus used some simple analogies to explain the Kingdom. It is always working, even though we can't always see it. Hidden, but real, living and active. Like yeast working through a batch of dough, permeating every inch, causing the loaf to rise. Like salt added to a stew, seasoning the whole meal so that every mouthful is full of flavour. Like a seed planted in soil that grows into a fully grown tree that provides shelter for birds.

This is how God can work through us. It doesn't always make sense to the untrained eye, but as we patiently and consistently offer God the little we have, He causes a marvellous, inexplicable acceleration of growth to take place and something tiny turns into something huge. It begins with the tiniest seed of faith.

MINDSET SWITCH

I've been privileged to witness many communities changed over the last two decades. The changes look different from town to town, but every case shares one thing in common: all that was required to get something started was the tiniest hint of a change of mindset. That's why I'm writing this book. To encourage people, just like you, to become possibility-thinkers in your community. To offer encouragement and practical guidance to help you turn away from the mindset that says, "This is the best we can do" and instead embrace, "Let's try something new." To replace the "drop in the ocean" mentality with a far more inspiring outlook. After all, an ocean is nothing more than many joined up drops of water.

In every case of community change there is a progression that takes place. There is a move away from initial wishful thinking, seasoned with lots of little doubts, towards enthusiastic agreement and an optimistic belief. From, "If only things could improve around here" to "Together we can really do this!"
The first step of this progression is one of realisation. A change of belief away from the thought that change can only come if some external, super-powerful agency steps in to rescue us, to the understanding that, in fact, the resources necessary for change already exist in our midst. Transformation starts when we use the little we have and ask God to multiply it. It is a significant adjustment. One that is perfectly illustrated in the New Testament through the story of the feeding of the five thousand – an account recorded by all four Gospel writers.

FEEDING TIME

The crowds of people who had swarmed out into the Galilean countryside to listen to the teaching of Jesus were becoming hungry. When the disciples reported this to their master he replied, "Well feed them then!" This is perhaps the most outstanding aspect of the story – the fact that rather than simply demonstrating his divine power to solve their problem, Jesus invites his disciples to participate with him in providing a miraculous outcome.

The immediate response of the disciples reveals their limited mindset. They immediately raise some practical concerns: "But, we're miles away from the shops! And, anyway, we don't have anything like enough money!" Later in the Gospels this kind of thinking is referred to as "the lesson of the loaves". We'll return to that in a moment. Suffice to say the disciples were novice "possibility thinkers". They didn't grasp at all what was unfolding before their eyes.

What's even more remarkable is that they still hadn't learned the lesson at the end. Despite having fed thousands and filled twelve baskets of leftovers, the disciples still failed to recognise the provision, followed closely by the protection, of God.

A few hours later they were caught up in another storm on Lake Galilee. This time they were alone and they saw Jesus walking on the waves. They were terrified! Not just by the weather, but by the sight of Jesus outside the boat. What's really interesting is that, at this point, Mark feels it necessary to come out of the narrative and make a comment. He doesn't go for the obvious link – that they'd been in a similar stormy situation before (Mark 4:35-41). Instead, he states that there was something within the feeding miracle that they had all missed. But what could it be? (Mark 6:52)

"Immediately he spoke to them and said, 'Take courage, it is I. Don't be afraid.' Then he climbed into the boat with them, and the wind died down. They were completely amazed, for they had not understood about the loaves; their hearts were hardened."

They had not understood the miracle and had still not grasped the power Jesus has to transform a situation. How often do we fail to learn from the way in which Jesus has delivered us from troubles in the past and that he can do so again? We will return to this idea, often referred to as the lesson of the loaves, later in the book.

The miracle occurred when a small boy with a packed lunch

volunteered to Jesus his meagre contribution in "feeding" the masses. In doing so, he perfectly modelled the ideal approach to partnering with God. "This is all I have," he seems to say. "Maybe there's a way of using this to solve the problem?"

This kind of attitude delights Jesus. He saw a similar mindset in the Centurion who told Jesus not to travel all the way to his house in order to heal his servant. "Just say the word," he commented "and my servant will be healed." Faithfulness like this delights God because it is an open invitation for Him to get the job done. Quite often the disciples, who should have known better, spoke with a different tone. They focused on the problem or the practical, rather than walking in faith and trusting God for his solution.

The lesson of the loaves then, is this: just as God provided food in the desert, just as he protected his people on countless occasions throughout history, he would do so again. They had nothing to fear. He would meet their needs and, at the same time, he would stretch their faith.

Christians who want to see their communities transformed can picture themselves present on that Galilean hillside. We're either sharing the same little glimmer of hope that something might just happen, since the Master is present, or we're pointing out the practical problems – all of which, of course, are perfectly valid reasons why change will be difficult. Yet the message of Christ to all of us rings clear: "If you want to see things change, get on and start the ball rolling."

Imagine how bewildered the disciples must have felt as they weighed up Jesus' words: "You feed them!" How could they possibly feed thousands of people when they had absolutely no food at all? Then, up pops this innocent lad with his naïve offer, which in their eyes only served to underline the scale of the challenge. Five barley loaves for five thousand men (women and children weren't counted). Oh, and let's not forget the couple of tiny fish. How on earth could this make any difference to the impossible situation they were facing?

Right here at the start of the story, before any of the drama unfolds, there is a massively important detail that may well hold the key to the whole miracle: Jesus didn't make something out of nothing. He made something big out of something small. He multiplied it. But it all started with what the boy gave.

On the surface, what appears to be negligible, in fact is very significant. A minute ago there was no food at all. Now there is some food. It's a start. A step in the right direction for those with the right mindset.

The challenge lies in how these limited resources are perceived. We can say, "It's not enough" or we can say, "At last, God has something to work with!"

MULTIPLIED

I wonder which disciple was the first to take a tiny handful of bread and fish from Jesus after He had prayed and blessed it? I wonder what thoughts went through his mind as he held his portion out to the first small group seated on the grass? I suspect he may have started out thinking that his involvement would be over pretty quickly. One small serving handed to a bunch of hungry people – end of story. Imagine his surprise when he discovered that he still had the same amount in his hands as he moved on to the next group. And then it happened again! It probably didn't take very long for him to experience the mindset switch. "Together we can do this!"

This is the heart of the challenge we face in community transformation. We need to make the mindset switch at the earliest possible point. We need to learn the lesson of the loaves. The moment the boy stepped forward with his contribution the whole picture changed. The possibilities were now unlimited. Here was some raw material for the Lord to make use of. The miracle had begun. In no time at all its impact was multiplying. The disciples must have grown in confidence as the seemingly hopeless situation was transformed.

How many times have you heard, "If only we had some money we could improve this community"? Or, "Why are there no facilities for our young people?" We need to make the mindset switch. If we start to think differently and exercise our faith, then the miracles can begin. We need to stop thinking and working along traditional lines and open our minds to the limitless possibilities for change that present themselves as we explore what is already happening in our communities and pray that God will bless and multiply it.

John follows his account of the miracle with the mysterious references Jesus makes about himself being the "bread of life". The feeding of the multitude was more than a meeting of people's immediate physical need – it was strongly symbolic of the spiritual "food" made available to all through Jesus.

The famous fifth century Bishop of Hippo, St Augustine, developed this thought further in his Eucharistic charge to the faithful, which tracks the pattern of Jesus' handling of the bread during the miracle:

"You are the Body of Christ," he declares to the faithful. "In you and through you the work of the incarnation must go forward. You are to be taken. You are to be blessed, broken and distributed, that you may be the means of grace and vehicles of eternal love."

In the same way today, we who follow Jesus can do more than merely partake of the bread of heaven, we can also participate in multiplication miracles of our own, in partnership with others – even those who may not share our faith in Christ (yet!), but who do share our desire to see communities transformed.

We can play our part and see God do something extraordinary. All we need is a seed of faith, a little bit of vision, a bit of courage to step up and have a go. And, of course, a change of mindset – to allow for the possibility that all kinds of resources, already in our reach, can, under His watchful gaze and in His powerful hands, be miraculously multiplied for the benefit of many.

QUESTIONS FOR DISCUSSION/REFLECTION

- Discuss "mindset" – having a positive, can-do attitude: is this personality? Faith? Cultural? (British? Middle Class? Christian?)
- List the good things about your community
- If your community were a person, how would you describe their characteristics? Friendly, generous, hospitable, suspicious, other?
- Has it ever occurred to you that many non-church people/ groups share a common desire to improve community life?
- How would you feel about working with them? What would be the challenges and how would you deal with them?

2

CITY-CHANGING PRAYER

Prayer is always at the heart of what we do in ROC, even down to the detail of where and how projects develop.

Those who know me well will tell you that I am passionate about prayer. The city-wide prayer movement that we started in Manchester twenty years ago has now developed into many expressions of prayer. I can always easily remember the date when it all began, since the very first Prayer Network gathering took place on the day our youngest son, Matthew, was born: October 23, 1993. Needless to say, after spending months preparing for the launch of the new movement, I missed the main event! Matthew is twenty-one in October 2014, so it's a good way to measure the passage of time and the growth of the prayer movement.

Our other son, Josh, is on the leadership team of a new expression of prayer, Prayerstorm (see www.prayerstorm.org), which takes place regularly in Manchester. He grew up in a household filled with prayer and an environment of encouraging others to join in. As a little boy he even remembers stuffing the envelopes with invitation flyers to Prayer Network. The style and format of Prayerstorm is very different – largely due to the fact that it's led by a team of young people – but the heart and the focus are the same: our society is turning away from God and his ways and the evidence is there for all to see. Only God can change things and he does it by changing people. Come Lord Jesus! Pour out your Spirit on this land and bring transformation to our communities. Not just a temporary touch, but lasting change; sustainable change – redeem our communities.

So, prayer is vital and one big lesson I have learned over many years is that effective prayers are those that have a specific focus.

ROUND AND ROUND IN CIRCLES

Before the invention of satnav I was regularly challenged when it came to directions and travelling. Even after the advent of digital maps, which point the way for us by giving very precise directions, I would still often find myself to be indecisive, especially on roundabouts where there are a number of exits. Rather than making a mistake and taking the wrong turn, I would circle the roundabout a few times just to make sure, to weigh up my options, to plan ahead. Sometimes this process could be both lengthy and comical. I have been known to go around several times before committing to a particular exit (and sometimes that's the wrong one!)

I'm reminded about these experiences when it comes to the subject of prayer. Prayer is often likened to a journey. It will have a few signposts along the way, which I will call "items for consideration", but there should be a definite destination in mind. We usually want to pray for something specific before we start out, just like we have a specific destination in mind before we put the key in the ignition. Why then, do our prayers sometimes feel like they are stuck on some kind of spiritual roundabout? Not really making much progress; maybe even going around in circles; not really getting to the place we want them to be. Sometimes it's all too easy to "circle around" offering the same old prayers with little or no focus in mind. It's like we either don't know how to move on or maybe we are simply too scared to do so. It's this issue that I'd like us to look at first.

PRAYER IS A POWERFUL FIRST STEP

There are at least two obvious implications when we refer to prayer as a powerful first step. The first is that prayer is a good place to start but it's only a first step – there will be further steps to take if we're going to see communities redeemed. We'll have to do more than just pray and then leave it all to God. When we start to pray for God to act, we need to believe that He listens to our prayers. Assuming our requests are in line with His will, we can expect him to respond in some way. So, as well as praying, we should also listen and watch for his response. As we listen we may well hear God speaking to us, telling us to do something as part of his plan. As we look around with expectant eyes we may spot an opportunity opening up that could provide part of the solution. If we're open to the leading of his Spirit, we won't be surprised when we find ourselves in conversation with someone who shares a similar motivation to see our neighbourhood enriched – maybe even someone who doesn't know Him ... yet! Prayer is the first of many steps.

Second, prayer is a powerful step. We can't explain it, but haven't we all experienced the power of God in and through prayer? Sometimes it's a tangible manifestation of the presence of God in our inner being: a sense of peace and joy, security and encouragement. On other occasions there's a feeling of conviction – something is out of alignment in our lives and the power of God makes us aware of it (and enables us to deal with it, as long as we're willing). When thinking about community transformation we can easily acknowledge that so much of what is needed is beyond our ability to deliver – hence we absolutely rely on the power of God to be at work behind the scenes. Church history is full of examples of major social change following significant movements of prayer.

An obvious way to start to pray for our community is by observation of the social need. It's not difficult to spot specific areas in society where things need to change. As I look back on those early prayer meetings in our city, it's really encouraging to see how things have indeed changed. The content and the focus of our prayer meetings today has altered because the circumstances are different now. I still find myself praying about the same root causes, but I have moved on in some of my thinking and practice. I've become more observant – both of the needs of my community, but also more aware of how God is meeting those needs. One thing hasn't altered though: prayer is always my first step, regardless of what's going on around me.

A few years ago my husband, Frank, and I were asked by a publisher to write a book which outlined how we had gathered people together over a ten year period to pray for spiritual transformation in Manchester. It was published in 2005 by Kingsway and called City-Changing Prayer (recently reprinted and available from www.roc.uk.com/shop).

The book not only records the exciting progress that was made in the way churches began to gather across the denominational divides to pray in large numbers for the city, but also offers transferable principles that could benefit Christians in other places. Some of what follows in the remainder of this chapter is distilled from the content of that book. But even if you have read it before, it will be good to revisit it briefly in this context of community transformation.

When we wrote the book we really had no idea of the next steps that God was going to show us. Looking back now, we can see how vital these principles were, not only to the stage we were at as a church in the city uniting in prayer, but also in laying the foundations for the tangible, practical action we're now involved in.

City-changing prayer (or town- or village- or neighbourhood-changing prayer) is not about personal prayer, important as that is, it's more concerned about the subject of corporate prayer:

- prayer that draws believers together across denominational boundaries and social divisions.
- prayer that bridges the generational gap, the culture gap, the gender divide.
- prayer that looks away from the needs of the church and the desires of the individual and focuses instead on the issues that affect the world outside – education, healthcare, crime, poverty, justice, entertainment.
- prayer that not only touches the lives of those outside the church in our towns and cities but also draws them in, includes them and involves them.

- The kind of prayer that celebrates the unity and diversity of the family of God, follows the agenda of the Kingdom of God, and spills over into action for the glory of God and the benefit of His world

What began with a handful of enthusiasts gradually, as the Lord guided us, grew into a movement that not only attracted thousands of ordinary Christians praying together regularly (ordinary as opposed to specifically gifted intercessors), but also birthed and supported all kinds of Kingdom activity from youth missions to MPs' breakfasts, to crime reduction partnerships with the Police and Government. A city-wide army of believers taking the battle to the enemy and seeing God grant some amazing answers – to His praise and glory.

We were not claiming to be experts by any means, but we had stumbled across a number of key principles that seemed to be of great importance.

We outlined and illustrated them in detail in the book, but I'd like to pick out just three to highlight here. These are the key elements of what we believe make up the distinctive outward thrust that God is seeking to establish in the prayers of his people as we focus specifically on making our neighbourhoods safer and kinder places in which to live.

1. VISION

The Bible says that where there's no vision, the people perish. In the Hebrew this literally means to "throw off restraint" suggesting a kind of aimless chaos. It reminds me of the comments in the Gospels where God's people are described as "sheep without a shepherd". A more recent saying is "those who aim at nothing are almost certain to achieve their aim." On the other hand, however, experience shows that where there is a clear vision, a great deal can be achieved.

Back in 1993, God gave us a vision of our city which was reminiscent of Nehemiah's Jerusalem, except that the broken walls were symbolic of the fractured morality of society and particularly the deterioration of community life. People were increasingly living separately from one another. In the vision we saw enemy armies swarming through the gaps in the city walls causing devastation and death. Dotted around the perimeter were strong towers that had resisted the enemy attacks and survived. As we prayed into the vision we sensed that these towers represented churches and Christian groups which had survived but were functioning in isolation: each doing their own thing with no consultation or cooperation. God was challenging us to call them together "to rebuild the city walls" through corporate prayer, which would change the spiritual atmosphere over our city and pave the way for the wholesale transformation of the entire region.

Very inspiring stuff indeed. But we also had a strong sense that the outworking would be gradual. The city would not be transformed overnight. We needed to be patient and be prepared for lots of small steps to be taken. God spoke to us from Deuteronomy 7:22 where his enemies were defeated "little by little" and his people inherited the land "step by step". It gave a welcome handle for many of us to hold on to. We've all heard exciting prophecies about sudden revivals and so on and I'm sure that some of them will come to pass. But for many of us, maybe trapped in our British cautiousness, the realistic nature of this steady progress was easy to buy into. Frank particularly liked this and referred to it as Middle Aged Man Vision!

Vision. If you haven't got it, don't try organising anything, especially if you need others to help you achieve it. Instead, get before God and ask him to show you the community as he sees it. Find out what's breaking God's heart, let it break yours also, then share it with others and watch the fire spread.

2. UNITY

This is a much-used word in Christian circles, but it has a wide range of different interpretations. For some, unity is forming a committee of representatives from different churches to organise the annual summer fete. For others, unity is where everyone closes down their meetings, denies their traditions, burns their statements of faith, sacks their elders or bishops and starts meeting together every evening in a football stadium. Well, unity does not mean unanimity or uniformity. It means mutual submission and preference, one of another. In fact, as Paul points out in Ephesians 4, we are already united: there's only one Church, one Lord, one faith, one baptism and so on.

But the thing is, although we're all one in Christ in the spiritual realm, from an earthly perspective the Body of Christ appears fragmented. That's why, in the same chapter, Paul urges Christians to demonstrate that one-ness. Ephesians 4:3 has the very strong imperative: "make every effort, [earnestly strive (Amp)] to maintain the unity of the Spirit through the bond of peace."

Jesus himself prayed for the Father to make the Church one – and he wasn't just talking about the disciples of his day but also future believers – you and me, two thousand years later. Christian unity is not an optional extra but a core component of the Kingdom. God is calling Christians in these days to pray and act together in a way that highlights the central truth of the Gospel and in a way that will allow his Spirit to flow out in power and love to a hurting world.

But it's not easy is it? Anyone who's been involved in any of the many attempts to get Christians together from across the denominational divides will know how excruciatingly difficult it can be – and how unfruitful sometimes as well. But, where the vision is clear and sound, unity is not only possible but also very sweet. "How good and pleasant it is when brothers and sisters dwell together in unity" (Psalm 133:1)

What we discovered in our prayer gatherings is that the key to uniting Christians in prayer is not to blur our theological differences but to celebrate them. We drew attention to the various styles of prayer available to us and urged everyone to respect and honour each other's preferences in the gatherings; even to have a go at praying in a new way to demonstrate genuine unity. On one occasion over a thousand of us were present in Manchester Cathedral and it was suggested that everyone knelt and prayed The Lord's Prayer together. For the majority in attendance this was a completely alien way of praying, but everyone knelt and joined in. Immediately a strong sense of God's presence fell upon the whole group. Everyone spoke about it later and the general consensus was that our unity had pleased the Father and what followed was the commanded blessing.

I am so grateful for the lessons we learned about demonstrating unity in praying for the city. It's a principle that applies just as much to our partnerships of community transformation as well. The key is to focus so strongly on the common purpose shared by all parties, that the inevitable differences on other matters fade into the background.

3. POSITIVE FOCUS

One aspect of corporate prayer that always raises questions is the subject of formal expressions of repentance. I have been involved in countless sessions of prayer where whole groups cried out before God on behalf of others who have sinned, either back in history (examples such as the slave trade or the Crusades) or in the present day (politicians, bankers) – the idea being that their actions incurred judgement and we can now become free of this by owning up vicariously.

Another challenge is the very negative analysis of our current world with all its immorality, godlessness and corruption. We are urged to pray against these manifestations of evil on the earth and even to "bind them" and "loose" the power of God in their place.

I am not going to debate these or other aspects of spiritual warfare. I am not against them and, as the Spirit leads, I believe we do need to be open to all kinds of prayer. However, I do prefer to take a more positive approach when praying for our communities. I find it more appropriate and more inspiring to focus on the good that already exists and pray for that to expand and increase. I believe God looks upon our towns and cities with pride and pleasure at the many expressions of beauty and goodness, as well as with sadness at where we let Him down. Like a parent watching over their children at work and play, so God wants to encourage us to keep on doing the good things and to do them even better. Isn't this how we train our kids to do what's right? If we're preoccupied with criticism and punishment to try and root out wrong behaviour we run the risk of producing unhappy, unadventurous children with suppressed creativity and joyless lives.

Yes, our towns and cities are wounded and ailing, but at the same time they're bubbling with potential. We need to see our community as God sees it, not reduce it to the cartoon images painted by the media where violent crime, drug abuse and prostitution dominate. Instead we need to see the full tapestry of education, art, business, healthcare, industry and so on – all of which the Lord is very pleased with. It was always God's will for people to form inter-dependent communities. The climax of history will be a city, by the way!

And every city, town and village on the face of the planet is made up of precious, creative, caring, hard-working people all made in the image of God.

Years ago I was impressed by the teaching of Pietr Bos, a Dutch theologian who encourages people to consider what it is that makes their community unique and distinctive. He taught that God had a redemptive purpose for cities and we could discover this by praying positively about the things that please the Lord in our neighbourhood.

We got really excited in Manchester when we began to see the picture emerging! Our city is strong and hardworking. It breeds industry (the first computer was assembled here; the Industrial Revolution was born in Manchester). Our city is musical and creative, artistic and full of humour. It's a no-nonsense, what-you-see-is-what-you-get type of city. It's supportive of the towns that surround it – nourishing and feeding many who depend upon it for trade. It's a youthful city, a sporting city, an international city, a growing city and so on and so forth.

Rather than focusing only on the many challenging social issues, we celebrated the good things and began to speak well of our city – the same way that you'd encourage a child to develop.

Have you ever thought to do that in your community? To celebrate the positive aspects of your town or city. Talk it up instead of running it down? Why not commit to giving thanks to God for all that's praiseworthy – the schools, the hospitals, the police force, the sectors of the economy that are doing well. Why are we so negative? Is it a racial thing? The Americans are the opposite, aren't they?! Why do we constantly whinge about the loss of our heavy industry and the closure of mines? Why can't we focus on the fact that our country is leading the world in information technology? Why don't we rejoice that our children have careers opening up for them that won't give them asbestosis and chronic bronchitis and a life expectancy of 50 odd?

One huge example of the benefit of praying with a positive focus happened in 1998 and would shape the future of ROC well before I had any notion of the kind of projects that would emerge in coming years. God called us to pray for the Police. This was at a time when the whole nation seemed to be angry with the Police over allegations of widespread corruption and racism. A public enquiry into the way they had handled the investigation into the death of Stephen Lawrence concluded that the force was institutionally racist.

We felt strongly that we ought respond in the opposite spirit and to pray positively for the Police, expressing our gratitude for their brave and tireless work on our behalf. We printed hundreds of A3 posters which we gave out to Christians all across Greater Manchester for them to take into local Police Stations and ask for them to be displayed in the staff canteens. The poster read:

We would like to say a big

THANK YOU

To all police officers and civilian employees of Greater Manchester Police. Thank you for serving our society with commitment, diligence and integrity. Thank you for affording protection to the vulnerable, and for your efforts to maintain law and order for the benefit of all people in our Region. **We are praying for you:**

- That God would be with you in your work and in your leisure.
- That He would protect you and your families from evil.
- That you would know Christ's peace in your hearts and minds.

With love and appreciation on behalf of the whole Christian Community of Greater Manchester, from the Core Group of Prayer Network (an inter-Church movement of prayer representing thousands of Christians from many denominations)

[details of the meeting and contact telephone numbers]

Back in those days we had no specific contacts with Greater Manchester Police, we just knew one or two Christian police officers. Little did we know just how powerful this positive prayer focus would be. The response we received from officers and staff across the region was overwhelming and very moving.

Over the next few years a strong relationship grew between the Police and churches and Christian missions groups, which led to grants being given to evangelistic missions out of crime reduction budgets (one of £50,000 to Festival Manchester, which was officially delivered in partnership with GMP whose logo featured on all the literature and publicity). Now, through ROC, we are working in formal partnership with dozens of police forces all across the UK and I regularly receive direct requests from senior officers to help connect them with local churches.

Similarly, we held a special evening of prayer for politicians and were surprised, as we interviewed them at the front, at just how wary they were! One MP told us that every single communication he'd ever received had been either a request for something or a criticism. When we told him that all we wanted to do was to thank him and pray for him his eyes filled with tears.

It's time we started to pray in a positive direction for our towns and cities, with an attitude of gratitude and an agenda of support. You'll be amazed what doors this sort of prayer can open for the advancement of the Gospel and the transformation of communities.

Manchester City Council used to be quite sceptical towards Christian things. Since we started to pray for the City Council rather than coming against the principalities and powers that are sometimes at work through their policies, we've seen the most incredible turn around. The council now approaches us to ask for help with youth work and social action.

Positive prayers lead to positive outcomes and God is glorified far more through the fruitful relationships that emerge.

A much-quoted verse in the context of corporate prayer is found in 2 Chronicles 7:14:

"If my people, who are called by my name, will humble themselves and pray and seek my face and turn from their wicked ways, then I will hear from heaven, and I will forgive their sin and will heal their land."

God will hear from heaven when we raise our voice as one and seek him on behalf of our communities; when we follow up our prayers with compassionate action in partnership with other agencies who share similar concerns. He'll come and redeem our communities through the active and prayerful participation of the Body of Christ, united in purpose and flowing together in the power of his Spirit.

Humbling ourselves as the people of God will certainly involve acknowledging other groups who are working towards community improvement, even if they don't (yet) recognise that they're serving the purposes of God.

Repenting may mean much more than saying sorry to God in a prayer meeting for the mess our community is in. it may even include getting involved in providing some solutions to the problems we're aware of and doing so in partnership with others – fellow believers and others. For our land to be healed it will need Christians to repent of our isolation from each other and our arm's length attitude to the problems of our communities. But, important as these active matters are, we must never lose sight of the need to pray. God hearing and responding from heaven is the key to community transformation. The healing of the land that we desire must come from him. Our best efforts alone will only ever meet a few superficial social needs here and there. What we seek can only be achieved by the Lord and his involvement can only be expected when we do as we're told.

Let us pray.

QUESTIONS FOR DISCUSSION/REFLECTION

- What specific, measurable changes do you have faith to pray for?
- How would you like your community to look in 5 years from now?
- How could you connect with others to pray?
- What good things can you "talk up" about your community?
- What are the keys to persevering in prayer?

Interview with Neil Wain, former
Assistant Chief Constable GMP

3 WHAT'S SO BIG ABOUT SMALL?

The crowds were hungry and the disciples were making excuses when Jesus said these challenging words: "You feed them."

The reaction of his followers is to see all the reasons why this simply can't be done. Where will they get the money to buy enough food to feed more than five thousand people? Getting the wrong end of the stick is their usual practice. Jesus points to an answer much closer to home. Somewhere in the crowd there is some food. "How much bread do we have?" he asks. They find a boy with his packed lunch. It's not much, just five loaves and two fish. Jesus takes what is offered, organises people to sit in groups of fifty and then multiplies what has been given.

We are made with unique gifts and talents which, if brought to God in faith, can be used and multiplied. I have learned this lesson many times and am still learning it today.

How often do we focus on the barriers and reasons why our own contribution is too small and insignificant to make any real difference?

SMALL BEGINNINGS

In Zechariah 4:9 we read the frequently quoted phrase, "Don't despise the day of small beginnings."

We ask, will the little I have to offer really count? Because we believe it won't, we often fail to do it. We have a tendency to dismiss or overlook the small things. We make the mistake of believing that our small contribution will not even scratch the surface of the presenting need, so we do nothing.

St Francis of Assisi once said, "Start doing what is necessary; then do what is possible and suddenly you are doing the impossible."

I like the story of Richard Branson. Richard was born in 1950 and at the age of 17 started publishing a student magazine. Three years later he founded Virgin as a record mail order company. He soon opened his first store in London's Oxford Street. Then in 1972 he formed the Virgin Records music label, growing to be one of the world's top six record companies in the 80s through popular artists such as The Rolling Stones, Janet Jackson and Peter Gabriel. Since then the Virgin brand has expanded into flights, rail travel, retail, the Internet, drinks, hotels and leisure, and finance. Richard Branson is a good example of someone who's learnt to take small beginnings and expand them into greater horizons.

The journey of a thousand miles begins with the first step. Never take that first step for granted, no matter how small it might seem. What could be the small beginnings in your life? God's will is that you expand from where you are. God will always give you a bag of seeds – the opportunities and possibilities of life. If you can learn not to despise the day of small things and rejoice in the future of great things, ahead there lies great blessing.

GOD USES WHAT YOU BRING

What we bring to God matters. It counts for something, however small. We are co-workers with God and what we bring becomes part of the miracle. Many churches are praying for revival, renewal and restoration, and often the expectation is that something will "drop" from heaven. We are waiting for God to move and sometimes there is not much faith that our contribution really counts.

In our experience of working towards community transformation with towns and cities across the UK and beyond, God multiplies what is brought to him in faith. The boy brought the loaves and fish – nothing spectacular – but it was the raw material Jesus used.

Small things count and each one of us can make a contribution.

START SMALL

Often when we're starting out, we dream of doing earth-shattering things and the thought of tackling them intimidates us. This is another reason to start small. Don't try to help everyone, just try to help someone. Even if you never get to do what other people consider to be "big things", you can find great fulfilment in doing right things. No act of kindness is too small to be worth doing. One leader writes: "Little did I realise when I started with a desire to add significance to others, that it would add significance to me! Now I understand. We should not receive anything without giving, and we cannot give anything without receiving."

Mother Teresa said, "We can do no great things, only small things with great love."

WHERE DO I START?

Start with the need and then identify the unique contribution you can make. These two things combined create the beginnings of a miracle of multiplication. In simple terms, people were hungry and the young boy brought his lunch.

Consider, for example, the needs of those who are older in life. In a recent national survey of over sixty-five year olds, one in three people said that TV was their only company and they felt lonely most of the time.

Or ask yourself, who do I know that suffers from some form of mental illness and would love a visit or just a phone call from someone to show they were thought about? (One in four of us will experience mental illness of some kind).

Or how about the challenges faced by many estates in the UK where young people lack meaningful activities and positive role models, which often leads to their engaging in anti-social behaviour.

Then there are what the government refers to as "troubled families", who face multiple problems at a huge cost to the community purse. Louise Casey, a government advisor, and someone who has been to several ROC events said, "None of us changes because we are given a report or an analysis. We have to feel that we want to change and know how to. Family intervention helps people to believe in themselves. Forget which agency you are from, remember the human being. What is missing in all of this is love" (The Guardian, November 2013).

There are so many social needs and we can't do everything. So where do we start?

MANDIE'S STORY

Mandie Munro started with the need she could see on her estate in Breightmet, Bolton. She also started small. She had to. The church she inherited, Breightmet Community Church, had gone through a series of problems. Disagreements between members had led to splits and numbers had fallen dramatically. In fact, there were only five people meeting together on Sundays, but she still believed that God was calling them to make a difference in the lives of those around them. Little did she realise that when she opened a ROC Café youth club in April 2012 it would become a thriving ROC Centre community hub in less than a year. Here's her story:

"I grew up in a happy loving family, but at the age of ten I went on my own pursuit of happiness and I was hoping to fill this empty gap I felt inside. Sadly I looked in all the wrong places. I lived in a small village in Scotland and I became the leader of a gang of local girls. By the time I was 11 years old I was hooked on drugs, which led to heroin addiction, and got me involved in small crimes like robbing people to get money for my addiction.

I began to realise that the more I did these things, the worse I felt. I was happy on the outside but more and more miserable on the inside. I tried to end my life and slit my wrists. I ended up on a life support machine. When I got out of hospital my outlook on life changed. I became a total recluse and I cut myself off from the outside world.

Several months later I ended up in hospital again, this time with a mystery skin illness. My body would turn black and blue and the skin over my eyes would swell so badly that I couldn't see and I would lie for days with cold bandages over my eyes.

It was at this time that I came in contact with a local Church of Scotland minister who would visit me every day and tell me about this guy called Jesus who could forgive me for what I had done. He told me over and over, "Jesus loves you" and every day before he left he would ask if he could pray for me. I thought this guy was crazy and I would laugh in his face and tell him where to go. One day when he came in I was so sick of him asking me I said, "Anything to shut you up. Just pray for me!" He did and went on his way. The next day I woke up with not a mark on my body – no swelling, nothing – the doctors were mystified.

Obviously, because of the visits from this minister, seeds were planted, but I wasn't convinced yet that God existed. However, I started to attend a local youth fellowship on a Sunday afternoon where we would gather to play pool and table tennis. A few months later we went to a Scottish community called Iona for a week's holiday. We thought we were going for a week of wild parties and it was a shock to find just a row of shops and an Abbey. I remember that it was Easter and there were special activities and speakers arranged. One evening we were in the abbey and a speaker was taking about this guy called Jesus again. Again I was hearing how much this Jesus loved me and could forgive me. The speaker then asked for anybody who would like to accept Jesus into their lives to go to the front. I got scared and made to run out of the Abbey. But somehow my legs took me in the opposite direction and before I knew it I was sitting in front of this guy waiting to be prayed for! Again, I got really scared and went to run away, but it was like I was stuck to the chair with super glue and I couldn't move. The guy prayed some more and this time it was different. I felt a deep peace that I had never experienced in my life before and I can honestly say from that moment onwards that I found the true happiness I was looking for in Jesus Christ.

I started to live my life for Jesus, serving him to the best of my ability. Life was still really tough and when I was 18 I was gang raped in an awful ritual that lasted over a complete weekend and also involved having a knife taken to my throat. Naturally after this you would think I might have turned my back on God, but it was the opposite: God was the only one I could share all my frustrations, hatred and bitterness with. My relationship with Him got closer and closer.

From the age of 20 onwards all I wanted to do was serve Jesus Christ. I wanted to give back to him because of everything he had done for me. I went to work for British Youth For Christ for two years and saw amazing things happen in the South Birmingham community I was placed in. Then I trained as a Methodist local preacher and had the opportunity to share the gospel in many churches.

I moved to Bolton where I became the minister of a church in an amazing community called Breightmet. We partnered with ROC in 2012 and the results have been astonishing. We started small with a ROC Café aimed at teenagers. Surprisingly, 50 youngsters turn up on the first evening – some of them stoned, drunk and very abusive. I told them they couldn't come in, but if they came back the following week in a sober state I would let them in. They returned the following week sober and have been every week since. In some of these young people we have seen major life changes for the better. One of the young ladies is now training to become a police officer and a young lad wants to be a lawyer. Some of them are now involved in leading the project! They have realised that being brought up on a deprived council estate doesn't stop their chances of reaching their true potential and this is something we keep on showing them at the ROC Café. We recognise this potential and channel it in the right direction.

Also, many of my volunteers' lives are changing beyond belief and they now testify to the fact that they leave their homes daily with a big smile on their faces as they set out to serve their community with love, compassion and kindness through all the projects we offer.

Since opening the senior ROC Café we have started so many new projects that we have become a ROC Centre and offer over twenty community projects every week. The ROC Café senior project is now open 3 days a week, plus we have a Junior ROC Café, ROC Football, ROC Wrestling, ROC Families, ROC Homework Club, ROC Arts and Media, ROC Create, ROC street Dance, ROC Drama, ROC 'n' Rolls Community Café, ROC 'n' Rolls Soup Kitchen and ROC Cinema. We are soon to launch ROC Laundrette, ROC Cycle, ROC Angels and ROC Care, working with the elderly and vulnerable in our community.

There is no greater honour than serving the living God and seeing my community transformed. We have had over 200 visitors from other parts of the UK, just coming to see what is happening here. All of the partner agencies are coming together and working with one another and community life has changed for good. I may have cancer at the moment, but I serve a healing, all-powerful God and every day I can get up and say, "But by the grace of God go I," as I have yet another day to experience amazing transformation."

Mandie has been recognised for the amazing work she does and has been invited to the Queen's garden party this summer. She is an inspiration to me and countless others who have met her through ROC events around the country.

The thing that stands out about her is how everything grew so amazingly from such small beginnings. The growth has been dramatic in terms of community transformation, with significant social and economic benefits. But also, lives have been changed for the better and her church has grown as a result, from five to seventy-five people in just one year. Mandie's own story has motivated her to do the work she does.

At the time of writing around 450 people use the centre every week for 20 different activities. It's always a very busy place to be with so much going on, and it's not difficult for anyone who visits to see the benefit this work is giving to its community. Since the project opened the local police have reported a 75% reduction in anti-social behaviour. This is having a much greater impact than just numbers on a piece of paper.

Ian Bailey, the borough commander for Bolton Fire and Rescue service, was among the guests at the first anniversary of the centre. He said he was delighted with the ROC Centre and its achievements. Ian reported that the number of serious and nuisance fires had fallen from 76 to 44 since the ROC Centre has been open. The cumulative economic value of this drop is a staggering £300,000. Malicious calls have also dropped by over 50%, which adds further saving of £13,790.

Fewer fires doesn't just mean fewer injuries or fewer strains on hospital A&E departments, it also means the reduction of unnecessary Police and Fire and Rescue personnel involvement. It frees up public services to meet the bigger, unavoidable needs of our communities. Ian also told us that in a recent call out, a local man was very hostile towards the fire crew (which happens a lot). He changed his attitude quickly when his son came out of the house and said, "Hey Dad, these are our fire officer friends from the ROC Café!"

Building relationships across agencies is at the heart of what ROC does. We know it makes a difference and, over time as attitudes change, costs are reduced, community cohesion improves and ultimately lives are saved. Ian is now keen to see ROC projects in other parts of Bolton and we are looking at how we can support that.

Small things, if done faithfully, can grow into something more significant than we could ever imagine.

Interview with Jim Battle, Deputy
Police and Crime Commissioner
Greater Manchester

To finish this chapter I have included some extra study material and resources to help us identify our gifts and take some steps of faith. Here's a short Bible study exercise that will help us understand the importance of using the raw material we have in partnership with God, and being privileged to witness the glorious outcome. You can use this on your own or as part of a group, in which case, the group activity will need a little advance preparation.

BRINGING WHAT WE HAVE TO GOD

In 2 Kings 4, Elisha the prophet of God is called on to help a widow. Her husband has died and creditors are threatening to take her sons as slaves. She cries out to Elisha for help on the basis that her husband both served the prophet and was also a God-fearing man. After hearing the widow's cry for help, Elisha asks, "What do you have in your house?"

The widow's response is very interesting. At first she comments on what she doesn't have. How tempting it is for us to focus on either our problems or our lack, rather than the potential of what we are in possession of. Sometimes, no matter how hard we stare, the glass just looks half-empty and the widow's first response to Elisha's question follows this pattern: it's a "half-empty" answer. "Nothing at all," she says. Then, almost as an afterthought, she mentions she has a flask of olive oil.

Crucially, it's after she's recognised what she does have that things start to change. Once the widow has identified her flask of oil, Elisha's instructions are clear: she is to do something with it. She is instructed to take as many vessels as she can and then pour the oil into them. A miracle takes place. From that small container, every single vessel is filled. The widow's resources are miraculously multiplied. Here are a few extra things worth noticing before we move on:

Firstly, the reason behind the miracle. We are rarely blessed purely for our own benefit. This miracle is no different. Of course, the widow has an urgent and immediate need, but her sons are also affected by the problem. If God is multiplying something, it's not usually for the exclusive benefit of an individual. We must always remember that God blesses us so that we can be a blessing to others.

Secondly, the miracle stopped when she ran out of vessels. Elisha told her, "Borrow as many jars as you can, from your friends and neighbours." God didn't multiply the vessels, he multiplied the contents. This was a community miracle. Anyone who lent an old battered jug or chipped pot also played a part. It's interesting that Elisha didn't say, "Find ten containers..." The scale of the miracle appeared only to be limited by the scale of her vision. Each and every container was filled, but none of the oil was wasted. It didn't overflow.

We always need to grow our vision and expectations. This story shows us why. If God is going to multiply something, we not only need to make sure that we've got enough containers, we also need to recognise what God may want us to use in the first place.

GROUP ACTIVITY

The prophet asked the widow, "What do you have in your house?" Recognising our resources is often a vital part of how we serve God and other people.

What skills and gifts do you have that you think God could use? It's sometimes awkward or difficult for us to identify these things for ourselves. This simple activity will help within a small group setting. Don't rush this. Dependent upon the group size it may take 20-30 minutes.

- Label an envelope for each person in your group. Each person takes a pen and a piece of notepaper.
- Each person writes about every other person in the group. Take time to think about the qualities, skills and gifts of those around you. You don't need to write your observations anonymously (unless you wish to), so you may decide to back up your observations by writing about times in your friendship where you've seen these qualities in action. Remember that we are looking to encourage each other. We are not looking for faults!
- Write on a separate piece of paper for each person.
- You don't need to write one for yourself.
- When you have finished, fold your papers and place them into the respective named envelopes.
- The last person seals all of the envelopes and then passes them to each person.
- Everyone should then be encouraged to take away their envelopes and read the contents privately, maybe a day or two later, when they feel ready. People may wish to do so as part of their personal quiet time and to pray first and ask God to speak through some of the things that have been written.
- Finally, when people read the contents of their envelope, they should look for recurring phrases or themes. A person's gifting is very rarely identified by just one person, so pay close attention to anything that is mentioned more than once. These things may especially be worthy of further prayer.

These resources might assist you further as you consider how your unique gifts might be put to work for God in your community:

- Network Gift Discovery Willow Creek:
www.willowcreek.org.uk
- S.H.A.P.E by Rick Warren (www.rickwarren.org)
- www.saddlebackresources.com

4

UPON THIS ROC

World renowned Church leader, Bill Hybels, famously said, "The local Church is the hope of the world."

What he means is that God's Plan A for communicating the Good News to people is in the hands of local groups of Christians. People find out that there is a God who loves them and has a plan for them to live life to the full, both now and forever, by having contact with those who already know him. Individual lives are redeemed as one believer shows and tells that Jesus is alive. By the way, there is no Plan B. Maybe that's why it's taking so long.

To take this a step further, whole communities can be redeemed as local groups of believers have contact with other local groups and show and tell that Jesus is alive. God's salvation plan is not only aimed at individuals. The whole cosmos is in view. God is reconciling all things to himself through the Cross (Colossians 1:20). As Gospel seeds are sown in a community, so the effects of the advancing Kingdom are experienced in many tangible ways, including reduced crime and anti-social behaviour among young people and a growing sense of peace and security among the elderly. This is salt seasoning society; yeast permeating community; a huge tree emerging and providing safety for the birds that perch in its branches.

We can't deny that we are living in a post-Christian country where most people have little or no knowledge of the God who loves them and sent his Son to die for them. A "Post-Christian" culture is defined as one in which Christianity is no longer the dominant religion and which has, over time, assumed a variety of values and world views from other influences (which may be an amalgamation of other religions' perspectives or none). The values of historically Christian societies have been diluted over time and the Church no longer occupies the position of centrality it once had.

In his article, The Church in a Post-Christian Culture, author Michael Craven writes, "In the age of Christendom, the Church occupied a central and influential place in society and the Western world considered itself both formally and officially Christian. So when we speak of post-Christendom, we are making the point that the Church no longer occupies this central place of social and cultural hegemony and Western civilisation no longer considers itself to be formally or officially Christian. This represents a monumental shift in the cultural context into which the Western Church is now attempting to carry out its mission. This raises two fundamental questions: What does this new cultural context mean for the Church and its mission? And, what exactly is the Church's mission?"

I believe that ROC is one of a number of models that – in a Post-Christian society – is helping to create a new cultural context that helps to ease local churches into authentic relationships that are mission-ready. Un-churched people are not sitting around asking, "What must we do to be saved?" A conservative estimate confirms that around 70% of people have no personal relationship with God. They don't attend a place of worship and have little or no reference points to the existence of God. Shouting slogans in shopping malls is not going to convince them of the truth of God's love for them or of their need for a Saviour. We need to find more appropriate ways to get people to discover that God is real and relevant – ways that recognise where they really are in their own thinking and in the context of our post-Christian world.

THE ENGEL SCALE

I first came across the Engel Scale about thirty years ago and found it really helpful in terms of recognising the value of nudging someone a little further along on their spiritual journey. It was developed by James F. Engel as a way of representing the journey from the point of having no knowledge of God through to spiritual maturity as a Christian believer. The model is used by some Christians to emphasise the process of conversion and the various decision-making steps a person goes through before they become a Christian.

"+5" represents someone who is a believer who is fully committed to Christ and this is reflected in the way they live their life. Someone at "-8" is aware of a Supreme Being, but has zero knowledge of the Gospel.

View the chart on the next page:

+5 Stewardship & service

+4 Communion with God

+3 Conceptual and behavioural growth

+2 Incorporation into Body

+1 Post-decision evaluation

NEW BIRTH

-1 Repentance and faith in Christ

-2 Decision to act

-3 Personal problem recognition

-4 Positive attitude towards Gospel

-5 Grasp implications of Gospel

-6 Awareness of fundamentals of Gospel

-7 Initial awareness of Gospel

-8 Awareness of Supreme Being;
no knowledge of Gospel

It's fascinating to me that, reflecting the prevailing culture of the 1970s when it was created, the scale only goes as far as minus 8, which accepts the existence of a Supreme Being. Today we need to add a minus 9 and maybe even a minus 10 to accommodate a large percentage of the population. The gap between society and the Church is getting wider and many people see faith as irrelevant. The idea of attending church would not cross the minds of a large number of people – some not even for the purpose of attending a wedding. This gap needs bridging and underlines further the importance of finding ways to meet people at this level with practical, tangible demonstrations of the reality and goodness of God.

ROC's mission, therefore, is to help get the Church involved more intentionally in this bridge-building approach; to help churches into the first stages of a mission strategy that invariably yields a bumper harvest. ROC is a Christian ministry 100% committed to and involved in the proclamation and demonstration of the Gospel of Jesus Christ. Every ROC project has a Partner Church. Other groups involved invariably include people who would not describe themselves as Christians. Typically, a ROC project will include volunteers from the local Police, Fire and Rescue, housing associations, residents' groups and so on.

What unites everyone at first is the common goal to see the community improved. As the project comes together and begins to develop, new relationships spring up. People connect and hit it off together. Friendships form and soon become vehicles for the love of God to be demonstrated. (By the way, we do sometimes forget and take for granted just how amazing it is to be on the receiving end of God's unconditional acceptance and love. Un-churched people are often stunned when they experience it first-hand). So ROC provides a platform to bring people together. Someone described ROC as, "A dating agency without the hanky-panky!"

As well as the hundreds of testimonies I've heard from young people who have come to faith through the ROC Café model and older people through ROC Care, I know of dozens of previously un-churched police officers, fire-fighters, local residents, council officials and so on who tell stories of being won over by their Christian co-volunteers who, over time, invited them to church events or Alpha courses, helping them to find Christ for themselves. I call it evangelism by stealth.

Stuart Murray's book, "Church After Christendom", published about ten years ago, has greatly influenced our understanding of evangelism. The first chapter, "Belonging, Believing, Behaving" is a challenge to churches to become more like God in the way we relate to not-yet-Christians. Our default position tends to be to want people to join in with our activities or meetings on our terms. In other words, they need to behave in a certain way before they can find out what we believe. Eventually, once they have learned when to stand and sit, not to smoke, how to dress and can recite the creeds and explain substitutionary atonement, we'll consider them for membership.

Yet God accepts people unconditionally. We need to do likewise. People are hungry to belong, but reluctant to trust that one way is right, coming from a pluralistic context. They therefore need to experience a "no-strings welcome" to be a part of our community redemption team. When that happens there is every chance that an openness to explore the Christian faith will follow.

Sadly, though, not all Christians see things this way. There are those who believe that proclamation must involve confrontation; that people need to know exactly how sinful and lost they are before discovering God's loving solution. Forgetting, for some reason that it is God's kindness that leads to repentance – and that rather than proclaiming judgment through a global skywriting campaign, he sent his Son to get up close and personal with us so that we could taste and see his goodness in everyday life – well-intentioned brothers and sisters will frequently challenge us about our subtle approach.

We held a large event recently in Glasgow's Royal Concert Hall to launch ROC in Scotland. The invitation had come directly from the Chief Constable of what was then Strathclyde Police (now subsumed into one national force, Police Scotland). The event was over a year in the planning and was well attended by almost two thousand people, the majority of whom were Christians who understand and welcome our softly-softly strategy to engaging with secular groups. Also present were hundreds of civic leaders, members of public services, local councillors, senior staff from housing associations, head teachers, NHS managers, celebrities from entertainment and leisure and so on.

The programme was carefully woven together to include examples of ROC's work in other parts of the UK (film material mainly, with short comments from project leaders and interviews with church leaders and volunteers), live interviews with church leaders, senior leaders from local government, the Police, Fire and Rescue and other secular agencies. One of the highlights was a live, unscripted discussion between the BBC's Sally Magnusson who was our main presenter on the night and Midge Ure, musician and local hero who co-wrote the Live Aid song, Feed the World with Bob Geldof. Midge talked about his own challenging upbringing in the toughest part of Glasgow and shared how impressed he was with the evidence he was seeing of agencies co-working to address today's social needs. Interspersed throughout were a few pure entertainment slots including the Police Scotland Pipe Band, the High School of Glasgow Chamber Choir, Graeme Duffin from Wet Wet Wet and his band-for-the-night, Ashton Lane and Britain's Got Talent winner Jai McDowall.

I was inundated with positive feedback after the event and I was delighted to hear that a number of our high profile guests had been so moved by the stories of transformation (including some clearly church-based personal ones) that they got involved in deep discussions with various members of the team – some lasting late into the night. One of our celebrity contributors said they wanted to waive their fee as they felt so impacted by the whole occasion. However, there were a few comments, made for all to see on social media, condemning us for not preaching the Gospel on the night. It was a "chance wasted", apparently, given the captive audience of so many not-yet-Christians and we really ought to have "presented a challenging message about sin and salvation".

I don't see it that way. The great thing is, bridges are being built between those who know the Lord and those who don't … yet. Teams of local people sharing a strong motivation to see neighbourhoods becoming safer and kinder places in which to live are working shoulder to shoulder in relationships of mutual respect. They are growing friendships that will open the way for authentic conversations about deeper issues. As long as Christians remain well prepared to answer questions about the hope that lives within us, these will prove to be long-lasting, fruitful Kingdom connections.

I was so encouraged recently by Bill Hybels' book, Just Walk Across the Room (Zondervan). We were studying it in our church over a four week period and I had been asked to preach on the opening chapter to start the series.

The title comes from an experience Bill heard about from a dinner guest. The man told Bill a story which demonstrated how vital these first stage steps are in evangelism. He had found himself standing alone at a drinks party in a crowded room and another man on the other side of the room, a complete stranger, left his group of friends and came over to talk to him. He simply walked across the room and began a conversation about nothing in particular. He had no agenda, he'd just noticed someone looking a bit lonely and walked across the room to make contact.

The two guys hit it off, finding a number of things they had in common and arranged to meet up for a coffee later in the week. They became friends and one day the issue of faith came up naturally in their conversation. The eventual outcome was that the man was able to invite his new friend to an event where he met Christ and was converted. Hybels' point is that, "just walking across the room" is the most important stage in the process. It's also the hardest part for many of us, because we're happy in what he calls our "circles of comfort". Most of our friends are Christians and most of our free time is spent with them. But how will we ever connect with those who need to know Jesus unless we step into the "zone of the unknown"? Once that initial contact is made we are in a position to be guided by the Holy Spirit in terms of what to do and what to say. It sounds a lot less stressful than most of the personal evangelism seminars I've attended and, from experience, I can vouch for the fact that it works.

Our "no-strings" policy of accepting and including people, both as co-volunteers on ROC projects and as beneficiaries, is definitely a key to the sustainability we are experiencing. Many good outreach programmes fail because the small core of volunteers become over-stretched. Often these are Christians who also carry responsibilities for other activities and there is a limit to their time and energy levels. Involving people from outside of the church family provides a broader base of willing workers, whose time can be shared out to suit their availability. Often, they bring experience of a wider range of activities and, sometimes, highly developed skills that can be used in the projects.

"No-strings" also means there is no expectation for anyone to attend church or engage in any religious activity as part of the project. Again, we do get criticised for not having a "God slot" in our ROC Cafés, but this can be another reason why many projects fail: some people are clearly labelled as "in" while others are not. Division of any kind causes damage, particularly among young people. The Partner Church offers all kinds of groups that interested people can attend if they want and those involved in ROC projects will be very aware that they are welcome if and when they want to find out more. The concept of unconditional, positive regard for all involved in a ROC project is one we guard jealously.

In addition, it is quite common for church projects to be rejected when applying for funding. Many grant-making bodies are simply not allowed to support anything deemed to be religious. A ROC project, despite being Christian-led, is regarded as neutral in this regard, since ROC's charitable objectives do not include the advancement of religion.

Many local people are attracted to ROC projects largely because of the non-threatening, multi-agency approach. They see the church working in partnership with the Police and others purely for the benefit of the community. We often hear "off stage" comments made by un-churched people about the church "doing what it should be doing for a change", which always makes me smile.

There are many wonderful examples of changed lives that come out of ROC projects. One such example is that of Carol, who happily gave us permission to publish her story:

Born in 1986, Carol suffered a seriously disturbed childhood. Her father openly had many affairs and she even had to call one of the women her "mum". When she was 4 years old she had the opportunity to go on the TV with her father, causing her mum to become jealous and claim that Carol was her father's favourite; even saying, "When your father dies, I hope you die with him." Whenever Carol was brought presents her mother would take them off her and throw them away. She remembers somebody buying her a beautiful doll and her mother threw it on the fire and Carol was made to watch it burn.

One of the women that Carol's dad had an affair with had a massive row with him and ended up killing him when he was drunk. Carol's mother then blamed Carol for this and constantly threw it in her face.

As a teenager Carol's mother got a new boyfriend who would physically and mentally abuse her and her brother, David, even training his dog to attack them. The couple would take the youngsters to cafés, but make them all stand outside and watch them eating.

Carol's first proper relationship with a boy began when she was 16. It wasn't long before he began to beat her, but she stayed with him out of fear. She became pregnant but her boyfriend was angry. He sat on her stomach and said I hope you lose the baby. He also stabbed her in the hand with a screwdriver – she still has the scars – and he threw scalding hot cups of tea over her head. She eventually escaped this abusive relationship after involving the Police and, for a while, things improved. But life was always a very bumpy ride for Carol. She subsequently had five more children from two successive relationships, both of which followed a similar pattern of abuse and neglect. One man told her that he had only slept with her because he lost a bet. Two years ago, with her self-esteem completely destroyed and her life a total mess, Carol, now a single mum of six with no job and no hope heard about the ROC Café. Her children had become involved and absolutely loved it, coming home full of excitement and falling over each other to tell her stories about these kind people who helped them with crafts and games. There was a policeman in uniform who played pool with some of the teenagers and had a laugh with them and next week a fire engine was coming for them to climb on!

Carol was intrigued and had to check it out for herself. She describes this as the turning point in her life: "From the minute I walked through the doors I knew my life was about to change forever. I found people who accepted me for who I was – they didn't try to pry into my past or judge me for the mess I had got into. For the first time in my life it felt like I had a family around me who genuinely cared about me and wanted the best for me." Like many other mums and dads from the estate, Carol became a volunteer in the ROC Café and began to organise and lead activities for the children. Her confidence grew gradually and she began to believe that life may have some positive things to offer.

One day Carol was called into the centre office by the leaders and she thought she was in trouble. In trepidation she sat down and waited for the bad news. She could hardly believe her ears when the project leader asked her if she would consider taking on the role of kitchen manager. She burst into tears. They were asking her to take on responsibility which meant that they believed in her. She would be trusted to look after money and stock. Even though it was still a voluntary post it felt to her as though she was taking on the most important job in the land. She took on the position and worked so well that the ROC Centre has now managed to find some funding to pay her. Carol is now renowned throughout the estate for her bacon butties and kind hospitality. She is adored by kids and adults alike and says she leaves her house every day with a huge smile on her face, knowing she is loved and valued and has purpose in her life.

Oh, and by the way, a few weeks before I wrote this chapter, Carol gave her life to Christ.

Watch the film clip

QUESTIONS FOR DISCUSSION/REFLECTION

• "Belong, believe, behave" as opposed to "Behave, believe, belong" – have you observed either of these attitudes in Christian groups?

• Can you see the benefits of ROC's softly-softly approach to sharing the Gospel, first by demonstration and only later by explanation as the opportunity arises?

• What do you think about the multi-agency approach to community transformation? What are the strengths? Are there areas of potential conflict – and if so, how could you prepare for them?

5
MIRACULOUS PARTNERSHIPS

One of the keys to community transformation is partnership working and collaboration. When various agencies including public services, local authorities, community organisations, churches and people who have a vested interest in community wellbeing work together, the results are much more fruitful. In ROC we refer to "people of goodwill" working together towards safer, kinder communities. This is one of the aspects of ROC which is unique. All ROC projects must have a Partner Church and must involve other agencies in a collaborative approach to meeting the needs of the local community.

Collaboration is simply defined as the act of working with someone to produce something. When we work together with a goal in mind we can often produce a bigger outcome than if we work separately. The whole is greater than the sum of the parts because of the extra potential that becomes achievable when ideas and energies are pooled.

Some of what we call "partnership working" fails to live up to this definition though. It could be that we have not identified or clearly articulated a goal or, if we have, it may have drifted from its central place in our activity. Perhaps because of minor issues being afforded too much attention or pressing matters crowding in from other aspects of the parties' everyday lives, aside from the project.

As an active and committed Christian for over thirty years I have to acknowledge that the Church and we Christians can be guilty of this. Recently I was at a meeting which included secular agencies and we were discussing hosting a community consultation. One member voiced his concern: "Will this just be another talking shop?" Sadly, I had to agree with his scepticism. In many cases, that would have been a good description. We have to move from talking to action.

As ROC has grown, our experience of partnership working with a number of agencies has developed. We have been recognised for our ability to work with public services and statutory authorities and our experience has highlighted some best practice to share with others. We have earned a reputation not only for being good at partnering with others, but also for our ability to draw groups together and help facilitate partnerships. This is particularly appreciated by the Police and local councils, who are intrinsically wary of relating to outside groups, having had many bad experiences in their history where well-meaning people offering their services not only proved to be ineffective and unreliable, but also (sadly, often including Christian groups) motivated by a hidden agenda.

Here are three principles for effective partnership working:

1. START WITH THE END IN MIND

True collaboration has an end in mind – it produces something. Church Networks and other similar forums and groups need a focus. One that is clearly defined, realistic and achievable within a stated time frame. Something more courageous than just "gathering." There was a time when just organising a group of churches to meet together and sing a few songs was a challenge, but surely those days have passed. We need to find ways of joining forces to deliver projects that demonstrate the love of God in action.

Networks need to coalesce around a clearly defined focus or outcome that the whole group adopts, so that there is agreement and a commitment to achieving what has been articulated. In the absence of a clearly defined outcome, a number of dangers emerge. For example, each member may have a different agenda that others don't agree with or are too polite to say so. Many church and civic leaders have shared with me that this is the very reason they don't join or stay in a network or group. It is why, historically, partnering with churches has been impossible because, they say, churches can't even agree with each other never mind statutory agencies.

We have many ROC networks and groups across the UK and have encouraged them to have clearly defined purposes and aims. The ROC Torbay group for example has developed a statement of purpose which defines its existence: "The ROC Torbay steering group exists to facilitate the delivery of ROC projects which meet proven social needs and complement the existing good work in the Bay. ROC projects aim to add value to existing work, rather than duplicating or competing.

It aims to:

- Promote the opportunities ROC provides.
- Support local groups who wish to set up ROC projects.
- Identify the gaps in terms of provision.
- Foster relationships with agencies that support the work of ROC.
- Support the aims of the wider ROC Devon and Cornwall regional steering group."

Having this simple statement enables the group to stay focused and achieve its goal. It has also made the group more accessible from the point of view of the agencies involved.

2. WIDEN YOUR NETWORKS

An observation of many groups is that their members are often all drawn from within a similar sector or stream. For example, the group consists only of church leaders or only of teachers or youth workers. Another is that many groups are narrow in terms of their demographic: predominantly male, middle class, well educated. There is obvious value in like-minded people spending time together, but real community collaboration is far more effective if we mix with those outside of our habitual social group. We need to ensure that the potential network of organisations being assembled to address the needs of our community represents as broad a range as possible.

Working in partnership with secular groups is a novel notion for some Christians. In the past, the very idea would have appeared foolish for a number of reasons. Firstly, many churches tended to favour a solo approach to projects, preferring to keep everything under their control. Even partnering with another church was a bridge too far for most. Secondly, it hadn't occurred to anyone that there may be a common agenda between the Church's task of advancing of the Kingdom of God, and the civic goal of improving life for local residents. Thirdly, secular agencies have traditionally been stand-offish at best towards the mission of the Church; at times, openly hostile in some cases. Nowadays, thankfully, many churches have moved into new ways of thinking about their mission and are more open than ever to cooperation with each other. In addition, the economic climate has forced statutory agencies to find creative ways of delivering the care and support for their communities they are committed to providing without the big budgets they used to have. The Church is suddenly viewed as a useful source of volunteer energy and doors are opening across the board for discussions about potential opportunities for collaboration.

3. AVOID TOKENISM

In observing the need to widen our networks, care must be taken to avoid falling into the trap of tokenism. Our desire to involve other people and agencies has to be genuine. People can easily spot when they are being included as a token representative. When people feel truly valued for who they are, the partnership works with a much greater impact. Our engagement with agencies must be genuine and that means we are prepared to listen to and learn from one another.

It's not easy to strike the right balance between making sure that a working group contains sufficient diversity without slipping into a politically correct mind set that simply includes a range of representation that looks the part. Anyone invited to participate must know that their involvement is genuinely valued and they are not just there to make up the numbers.

It's vital to involve potential partners in planning a project from the earliest possible stage rather than, as often is the case, inviting them along to rubber stamp what we have already decided to do. Again, this is a risky strategy, since different groups have different ways of thinking and acting. However, with patience and genuine mutual respect, a strong sense of agreement can be reached when everyone shares a common goal to begin with.

MIRACULOUS PARTNERSHIPS

When I talk about our experience of working across many agencies I often refer to the story recorded in Luke Chapter 5. Jesus speaks to a group of disillusioned fishermen who have been up all night and caught no fish. Luke records for us in verse 2: "He saw at the water's edge two boats left there by the fishermen."

Jesus gets into one of the boats and begins to teach the crowd. We're not told anything about the theme or content of the teaching. Maybe it was about faith. Or perhaps the need to persevere in the face of difficulty. Or just a simple reminder of how the Father provides everything we need. In light of Jesus' closing pronouncement, "From now you'll be fishing for people," it could be that the teaching was about preparing for the imminent influx of men and women into the family of God through the ministry of the master and his new team.

When he has finished, Jesus tells Simon to go out to fish again. Typically, Simon responds with a mixture of doubt and faith. He seems to say that as the experienced fisherman he knows better, but he is quick to submit to the master. Luke uses the word "miraculous" to describe the result: a miraculous catch. Presumably, he was thinking of the sheer quantity of fish, or perhaps merely the sudden presence of fish where there had been none just hours before.

I love the fact that, without the partnership element, this miracle would not have been completed. Simon and his crew were overwhelmed when they tried to haul in their nets but thankfully, their partners were standing by and were able to respond quickly to the signal. Between the two groups they were able to land the catch and everyone was filled with awe.

Imagine how different the outcome could have been. If those in charge of the other boat had only ever been nodding acquaintances, who didn't take much interest in Simon and his crew, they wouldn't have understood the signal requesting help. Or, if they had been negatively disposed towards them, they might have simply ignored the signal that beckoned their assistance. Watching them struggle may have been a source of amusement. The story in Luke could have been known as the disastrous sinking of a boat, rather than anything miraculous at all. Thankfully though, there was a relationship in place between the two boat crews that pre-dated the occasion. They were probably good friends and had frequently spent time fishing together. They may have developed a system of signalling across the open sea when one boat needed the help of the other.

I often preach from this passage to inspire Christians to seek out partners who can help us achieve our mission. Miraculous partnerships don't just happen, they need to be consciously developed over time and the onus is very much upon us, as custodians of the Gospel, to be on the lookout for opportunities. If we will take the time and trouble to look around in our communities we'll discover that there are plenty of people of goodwill with a similar heart for change. As we invest in building bridges of cooperation we'll find partnerships emerge that prove to be miraculous because of the great impact made in the community. Even partnerships that perhaps appeared unlikely at first – who would ever have imagined that churches would be linking up with the Police to demonstrate the love and power of God to their neighbourhoods? I have to pinch myself sometimes when I look around the country and see ROC partner churches collaborating so brilliantly with the Police, Fire & Rescue, housing associations, local councils and others – so many of whom would not have considered working with churches a few years ago. The truth is that these really are miraculous partnerships through which God's kingdom is having its uniquely miraculous effect in bringing hope and healing to hurting communities.

Our experience of working together with secular agencies over the last fifteen years has been very fruitful in ways we could have guessed, but also in ways which have astonished us. Miracles of provision have become an almost daily reality in ROC, but I remember back to how God provided our first rent-free building miracle. Here is the story of our first community centre which we call a "ROC Centre".

THE ROC CENTRE IN RADCLIFFE

ROC had been developing links with various agencies across Greater Manchester for many years and we were known as an organisation that had a proven track record in reducing crime and improving community wellbeing. So when the Council was forced, by the economic pressures that were sweeping the country, to close down three-quarters of all Council-run youth services they approached us to ask if we could help by taking on the responsibility for one of their community centres, formerly known as the Y Zone.

I remember the conversation well. They said, "Unless someone else can take the centre on, we'll have to close it down. We simply have to save money and we can't afford to keep everything going." We were delighted that we were held in sufficiently high regard by the Borough Council and excited at the prospect of being able to deliver a number of new projects through one location. At the same time, however, it would require a lot of extra work and would bring greater risk than we had previously taken on, in terms of carrying full responsibility for a large building.

As I weighed up the pros and cons I had a strong sense that God was giving us a great opportunity to make a greater impact and that I needed to grasp it as such and not be too daunted by the fact that we would have to find extra income to pay for rates and utilities as well as finding local volunteers to run the centre. To cut a long story short, we took a plunge of faith and offered to take the building, as long as we could be assigned a long lease. The Council had originally suggested a short lease, but agreed to a ninety-nine year, lease with no rent to pay.

As though this in itself was not sufficiently miraculous, we were also granted full exemption from rates (rather than the usual charity discount of eighty per cent) and the Council also offered to hire back part of the building from us to use for other services. In short, the facility runs effectively for one tenth of what it used to cost. Here is the story of how things developed.

The ROC Centre in Radcliffe is a vibrant community hub at the heart of the Coronation Road estate. This area is an Urban Priority

Area and is within the top 10% of most the deprived wards in the UK. The project is an example of effective partnership working between a number of agencies including Bury Metropolitan Borough Council, the Police and Fire services, the tenants' and residents' association and two local churches.

The ROC Centre opened its doors in October 2011. The Neighbourhood Police Team started daily Police surgeries in mid-October, offering two hours per day where local residents could call in to speak with local officers to report crime, concerns and other issues. After the first two months, over 150 pieces of intelligence and information had been received by the Police which would otherwise have remained unreported. This information led to a number of significant arrests, the closure of three cannabis farms and the resolution of some neighbour disputes.

The ROC Centre has achieved so much in a short space of time. The Police have reported a positive shift in public confidence as a result of the increased visible police presence on the estate and rapid response to information received through the daily police surgeries. Greater Manchester Police (GMP) crime statistics show a thirty-five per cent drop in anti-social behaviour (ASB) and a twenty-three per cent reduction in rowdy and inconsiderate behaviour in the area since the opening of the ROC Centre.

PROJECTS

The ROC Centre is home to several ROC projects, including ROC Football and the ROC Café Youth Club, and hosts a weekly bingo session run by the local Tenants' and Residents' Association. This two-hour activity on a Thursday afternoons sees fifty elderly residents attending every week. The session provides a social activity for many pensioners who rarely get out of their homes and are often lonely due to lack of social contact. When asked recently why she comes to the ROC Centre a local resident replied, "It's the highlight of my week."

The same community group also runs a low cost, bi-weekly luncheon club in the ROC Centre attended by dozens of local elderly people who all speak in glowing terms about how ROC has helped them make new friends. The ROC Centre hosts a short break for carers of young people with disabilities and learning difficulties.

In December 2011 the ROC Café opened in the ROC Centre. The ROC Café is a weekly diversionary activity for young people aged 11-16 years. The activity is run by volunteers and supported by staff from GMP Radcliffe Neighbourhood Police and GMFRS Whitefield Station. Volunteers come from churches and community backgrounds and bring a wealth of skills, expertise and knowledge in working with young people. ROC Café currently has a weekly attendance of around a hundred young people. The sessions are drop-in style with a range of activities including table-tennis, pool, board games, Wii, crafts and cookery. The sessions are free to attend and open to all young people attending High School.

When asked why he comes to ROC Café one young man responded, "I like to come because it's safe and I'm protected from people who want to hurt me." Another said, "Because it's fun and I get to make new friends."

Another activity, ROC Football, was launched at Radcliffe Borough FC in 2012. This is another diversionary activity for youth aged 11-16 years. The 5-A-Side activity is led by the

Radcliffe Neighbourhood Police Team and supported by ROC Café volunteers. There are currently 130 young people registered and it has a weekly attendance of 60-70. ROC Football is free and open to all young people in High School. Here's what the kids have to say about it:

Brad: "The reason I attend ROC Football on a Friday night is it gives me something to be part of and gives me something to do. If ROC Football wasn't there on a Friday night I would be hanging out on the streets with my mates and getting in trouble with the Police, because there would be nothing else to do and I would be bored. I also play Rugby at the weekends for Sedgeley Park Rugby Club, so taking part in ROC Football helps me to continue to build on my fitness. The ROC team are really great and have helped me work on some anger problems. This has helped me, as Andrea and Bez [two of the leaders] have given me their time and also let me help as a young leader at the ROC Café Junior project on Tuesday nights. I also take part in the ROC Café on Thursday night and Bez has let me run the music lounge which I really enjoy doing."

Darnel: "ROC Football gives me the chance to play football with all my mates on a Friday night. If I didn't I would just be sat at home in my room playing on my PS3. I also go to the ROC Café on a Thursday night where I can chill with all my mates, play pool, DJ in the music lounge and have the best chip butties made by Philip and Les. I really enjoy going to both ROC Football and ROC Café and both the teams are really great."

And one of the volunteers:

Darren: "I have now been volunteering with ROC for almost 3 years. In the time I have been a volunteer I have been involved in many of the projects in Radcliffe. I have built good relationships with the young people who attend each of these and have seen many of them start to develop into young adults. I have been heavily involved in ROC Football, taking a bigger role in this particular project. It has helped me grow in confidence and develop new skills. I believe myself and the team of volunteers will take this project to the next level and create even more relationships with the young people in the future."

In March 2012, Bury MBC Adult Care Services Learning Difficulties and Disabilities Team opened a base in the ROC Centre. Some of the team work from the centre during the week with a small group of adults with significant learning difficulties. All the supported adults live in the area close to the Coronation Road estate. The group are able to interact with other users of the ROC Centre. They join in the community lunch and bingo and they are learning a range of independent living skills such as cooking and money management. As well as using the ROC Centre as a base they are learning independent travel skills using the local public transport networks to travel to the centre and go out on trips.

Anne Stansfield, Manager of the service says, "The ROC Centre base is helping the adults become more confident in their own community, developing their independence and promoting inclusion of people with disabilities in the local community." This theme of increased self-esteem is repeated throughout all our ROC projects. The direct beneficiaries often tell us how much their confidence has grown as a direct result of their involvement and the same comments are frequently made by the volunteers and staff who do the work. Here's what Daniel wrote about how much his own life has been impacted positively through his work at the Radcliffe ROC Centre:

"I have spent most of my life living in a little town called Radcliffe. I come from a very good family background. However, as I started to grow into my teens, my Dad turned from being my best mate and my hero to being physically and emotionally abusive. I was told I was no good; that he didn't love me and that I wouldn't amount to anything. This had a big effect on my school life and my life in general. I became a very angry and sometimes violent young person. I fought through most of my teenage years and school life. I also started to try and fill the gap with sex, drugs and again, more fighting. This led to me getting a very bad reputation and I later found that my so-called friends were laughing at me rather than with me, as well as at times being scared of me too.

As this was happening I was still involved in church family life, but never really had a relationship with God. As well as my Mum and Granddad, there were also a few people in my church who believed in me enough to keep me involved and they steered me towards helping out with the youth and children's work through the church. When the ROC Café started I was asked if I would like to volunteer. I was moved to tears and threw myself fully into the work and got involved in everything I possibly could.

I know that if there had been something as good as the ROC Café when I was going through my teenage years it would have changed the way I looked at things. Even though that wasn't to be, I have still benefited through the experience I have had of helping young people dealing with the same problems I had. I see so many young people experiencing the feelings I felt at their age, and just like I was given the chance to make a better life, I want to give them the chance and hope that I can be a real influence and a positive role model for them. I see a need and feel I have to help make that change and show these young people that they can amount to something good and they do have potential and that people really do care about them.

I now have a paid role working for ROC and I am growing even more as a young man and speaking with many young people right across Manchester, befriending them and making a real difference; giving something back to the community and developing new partnerships and relationships all the time. I would like to personally thank Debra for seeing the potential in me and giving me an opportunity to make a small, but I hope a significant, difference to many young people's lives."

The ROC Centre in Radcliffe was the first of many that are now springing up in other locations. Other ROC Centres have started or are in the planning in Torbay, Glasgow, Newton Stewart, Chelmsford, Launceston, Trafford, Bolton and Leicester. We have a vision to see the model replicated in other communities because it works. The idea is only possible because of miraculous partnerships which enable the multiplication of resources and achieve a greater impact.

QUESTIONS FOR DISCUSSION/REFLECTION

- Why is it easier to work in groups which are made up of people like me? And how can I break out of my comfort zone?
- One of the fears of working with other agencies is that of compromise. Will we need to compromise our beliefs to work with others?
- Why is the multiplication effect possible when we work with other agencies?
- What do other agencies have to offer which we don't have already?
- When have you see a greater impact in terms of results achieved as a result of agencies working together?
- Are there any negative aspects to this kind of multi-agency work?

6 ROC CONVERSATIONS

Over the last few years we have developed a community consultation event called a "ROC Conversation" and, having now held hundreds of these, have learned some lessons about effective solutions to community needs.

The consultation focuses on specific geographical areas where there are social needs. It brings together members of the local community, including representatives from churches, faith groups, the Police Service, Fire and Rescue, the local authority, MPs and other agencies. Over time we have developed a successful model and have the expertise to offer agencies who wish to engage with their local community, sustainable solutions to local needs.

A ROC Conversation is both the culmination of and a catalyst for local visioning and partnership building for community transformation. It has consistently proven to be the perfect vehicle to create new possibilities and accelerate progress towards achieving goals for crime reduction, community cohesion and general community wellbeing. With appropriate preparation and follow-up, a typical ROC Conversation will achieve the following:

- A fresh, comprehensive and ambitious vision for the future of the local community that covers a full range of wellbeing objectives that address the priorities of local people, statutory agencies and businesses.
- Recording a more comprehensive catalogue of existing community assets than was previously possible.
- Creating a strong, shared purpose for the transformation and improvement of services, with an unprecedented level of co-creation with and commitment from all partners.
- Generate new ideas for change, drawing on the creativity and assets of the local community as well as on the new possibilities generated by deeper, cross-sector partnerships.
- Create new opportunities for collaborative working between statutory agencies, businesses, faith and community groups and local people.
- Generate new opportunities to release and maximise the value of community assets and volunteering.

The first step is getting everyone to agree to be part of it – which is quite a challenging piece of work on its own. Finding the right point of contact is quite tricky, especially as personnel in public services and local authorities are moved around a lot. Since we have such a good reputation with civic and public leaders, however, we are generally able to find people quickly and gain support for the idea. Community consultations are not a new idea, far from it, but agencies appreciate having a neutral umbrella organisation in ROC. They say there are a number of reasons why they prefer using our services:

1. **Rent-a-crowd.** Traditionally, community consultation events are very poorly attended and agencies can get quite discouraged, whereas we always manage to gather a crowd of, on average, about one hundred people.

2. **Handling the usual suspects.** It's a bit of a stereotype, but people who like to moan love the opportunity to attend community meetings to complain about dog fouling or cracked pavements. As important as these matters are, we tend to attract people with a wider interest; people who say positive things and want to be part of the solution. We also know how to strike the right balance between inviting and allowing people to make a contribution while minimising the impact of negative comments. It surprises our partners how frequently we see people change their attitude for the better during a session in which they have been listened to and thanked for their input as part of a wider debate.

3. **Getting the church involved.** ROC Conversations include the church in the list of invitees and church members usually form a good percentage of those who attend. Churches have a strong volunteer culture and are usually well motivated to help (that's what I tell the agencies anyway! And, mostly it's true).

4. **Facilitating group work.** Discussions are well facilitated by trained ROC staff using questions such as "What are the social needs of my community?" "What resources do we have at this table to get projects off the ground?" and "What could be achieved better by working together?" Sometimes the questions are more focused like, "If a ROC Centre opened, which needs would it address?", "How can we involve young people in the project?" or "How can we reach the elderly people in our community?"

5. A clear focus on the desired outcome. A ROC Conversation focuses on the outcome rather than on the problem. We have a clear plan as to how we make sure that outcomes are achieved within a specific time frame.

6. Matching of needs with the resources available. What do people have to offer? Skills, expertise, finance, knowledge, volunteers, buildings, equipment and time. We ensure that skills meet need in the most practical way.

7. Action groups. Often a local enabling group is formed to carry things forward. The group is made up of key people from a variety of organisations, typically: Police, Fire and Rescue, housing associations, churches, schools, the probation service, youth services. The group meets about once a month to ensure the aims are achieved.

Following the ROC Conversation we produce a report, which includes comments people have made, the socials needs which were considered to be the most pressing and detailed action points agreed at the meeting. The report is sent to everyone who attended as we always take contact information from every delegate. The report enables each member to be a part of the follow-up process, although I admit it takes a lot of work on our part to ensure actions are followed through. Setting up an enabling group or having one or two key leaders in place is the key to the next stage.

ROC CONVERSATION CHELMSFORD

The first ROC Conversation in Chelmsford, Essex, took place in November 2013. It was hosted by our friends Nicki and Pete Sims from CGC (Christian Growth Chelmsford) and attended by around one hundred and fifty people including the Assistant

Chief Constable of Police Maurice Mason, Deputy Police and Crime Commissioner Lindsay Whitehouse, Spencer Clark from Community Safety, Lee Markwick from the Fire and Rescue Service, Superintendent Nick Morris and Chief Inspector Ed Wells.

The evening had a great atmosphere and it was amazing how much effort the church had put into the organisation of it. We were treated to great refreshments (always a good move). They had also put together a welcome team, organised the room really well and even had a choir performing popular covers. Members from various agencies spoke about local needs and the group work unpacked these in more detail. It was fantastic to hear a report from the first ROC Café youth project in Essex, based in Stanford Le Hope, which started a few months ago and had already had to be re-located due to the growing numbers of young people attending.

The evening finished and our team went back to the hotel on a high. But it wasn't over. The next day as we met over breakfast to debrief with the guys from CGC, we had a visitor. The Police and Crime Commissioner Nick Alston, who was meant to be off for a week's holiday, had heard about how well the meeting had gone the night before and decided to join us for breakfast. He said he would be keen to support any next steps. After breakfast folks from the church took us around the town centre and we looked at a building which could house their ROC Centre. At the time of writing, there are discussions underway with the owners.

An action team has now formed under the banner of ROC Chelmsford to take things forward and I am convinced they will achieve some great results in the coming months and years.

Interview with Rob Groves from
Stanford Le Hope ROC Café

ROC CONVERSATION PARKHEAD

Ian Wills, the leader of the Church of the Nazarene in Parkhead, Glasgow, has been a good friend for a couple of years since he joined the working party to plan towards the launch of ROC in Glasgow in February 2014. He was undertaking a huge building project for his own church, but still gave his time to support and encourage us for the event at the Royal Concert Hall. His real passion, however, lay in his own back yard and he always had an inkling that he might be part of a ROC project in Parkhead. So in November 2013 he hosted the first ROC Conversation. Lawrence Bettany, our ROC National Projects Coordinator, travelled up to Glasgow to help facilitate the discussion. Members from various agencies were invited to Ian's shiny new church building (very impressive) and they started to dream and talk.

Ian is one of those people who, once they have decided to do something, doesn't hang around. So in January we squeezed in another ROC Conversation. I was there myself and it was a great thing to see. Sixteen different agencies attended and the sense of community, agreement and determination was noteworthy. A ROC enabling group are now looking at all sorts of possibilities, especially as they have the Commonwealth Games (Summer 2014) on their doorstep. The enabling group is made up of Jim Cavanagh from Fire Scotland, David Wilson from Parkhead Housing Association, Sergeant Chris Hoggans, Ian Wills from the Nazarene Church, Lisa Adair from Playbusters and Amanda Clark from Glasgow Life.

We are excited about the possibilities in Parkhead. It's a challenging place with many social needs. The night before our event there, a young man had been shot just around the corner from the church, a stone's throw from the new Commonwealth Games stadium. But it's also an area bursting with potential for transformation, as evidenced by those present at the event. As we often observe, in areas with the greatest needs, God frequently raises up people of great vision and capacity. I came away with a strong sense of confidence that this keenly committed group, full of hope and promise, would see exciting outcomes as a result of their partnership.

Interview with Ian Wills

Interview with Sergeant Shona MacKay

JUST DO IT

Last summer I had an interesting conversation at the end of a ROC Conversation in Launceston, Cornwall. As I have said, the really important part of all this is to identify the solution and implement it. Many community consultations fall at the first hurdle: they fail to implement a strategy which has been discussed and agreed upon. Or they fail to follow up on the action points raised and agreed during the consultation process. Some even omit to record any action points.

There is also sometimes a tendency to prolong the consultation and mapping phase. It's a typical human tendency: we love to analyse and theorise – it's easier than planning and acting. This came up in the feedback section following the group work in Launceston. There was a suggestion that more research was needed before we attempted anything new. That we needed to map the existing provision to avoid duplication and taking resources away from established projects.

It's a valid point but in my experience such suggestions are often a delaying tactic. I have seen myself, when revisiting locations years later, that frequently things have not progressed. I remember the Launceston discussion. I found myself saying that more mapping might not be the answer or at least we should consider exploring the new ideas at the same time. Gateway 2 New Life Church were hosting that night. They already had a vision to start a community hub, but were very mindful of not wanting to steam ahead without including others. I remember saying that my experience working with the public services has taught me to develop a "can do" attitude. The Police approach is: if it needs doing it should be done today. In ROC we have therefore adopted the well-used phrase "Just Do It". There comes a time when we have to move from mere vision to concrete reality. I could see the police officers in the room that night with beaming smiles, obviously agreeing. So did the leaders of Gateway 2 New Life Church. Just nine months after the event they have opened the ROC Community hub in a 10,000 square foot facility right in the centre of town.

At the end of the meeting Sian Hobson from Riviera Christian Centre in Torbay came to talk to me. She and her husband Paul had been leading a ROC project for a while and were starting to see results. She said that she liked the phrase "Just Do It" because it was working for them.

STORY FROM TORBAY

Paul and Sian lead an Elim Pentecostal church called Riviera Christian Centre on the Great Parks estate in Torbay. They have been there for fifteen years and have seen some really good community engagement. Since partnering with ROC and opening their first ROC Café youth project in March 2012, they have seen great results both in terms of community links and effective youth work.

Great Parks, formerly known as Queen Elizabeth Drive, is a challenging estate. The Riviera Christian Centre has set up three ROC projects: ROC Café for 11's-14's on Thursdays from 3.30-5.30pm, followed by a ROC Café for 14+ year olds 7.00pm and a Mini-ROC on Mondays for 5-11's.

Previously there was nothing on the estate for young people. Official figures from the Police report a fifty per cent reduction in crime and ASB since the project opened. Police Commander Jim Nye, speaking at a ROC Torbay meeting, reported that the Police would usually receive three or four phone calls every day from the estate and now they never get any calls and the "estate is not on their radar any more."

The Great Parks ROC Café projects are the result of collaboration between various agencies including the church, Police, Fire and Rescue, Children's services, Sanctuary Housing, Great Park Community Association, street wardens and Torbay Council.

Sian and Paul are excited by their links with ROC and Paul has recently told other Elim churches nationally about the benefits of partnering with ROC. Paul plans to plant out a new ROC project in Foxhole, a neighbouring estate, which will be ROC Care – a lunch club aimed at supporting and befriending elderly residents.

Paul says, "ROC has brought us into a place where we've had a brilliant opportunity to work alongside other agencies and it has given us a greater influence in the community. We also have the ability to measure results more effectively and have access to information and resources we wouldn't have had without ROC." New projects have started in the last year. As well as the ROC Café and Mini ROC Café there is ROC Football, ROC Bambinos and talk of more initiatives.

Paul says, "We have also been approached by Gail Rogers (Head of Integrated Youth Services in Torquay) to set up a Buddying Support project that pairs up parents who are coming out of the higher stages of support in Social Services, with volunteer support workers through ROC. The volunteers would be trained by Social Services and the parents would be referred to the ROC Team. We were thinking of calling it ROC Buddy. I can also see scope for a ROC Cook 4 Life course and a luncheon club in Great Parks to act as a meeting point."

The committee are discussing the possibility of becoming a ROC Centre which they say is the next logical step. The life chances of the people in Great Parks are being significantly improved now that the church is addressing their needs and improving the living conditions of their neighbours. Where you live doesn't have to limit your potential. Location is an important factor, but with people like Sian and Paul around the odds can change.

Interview with Paul & Sian Hobson

Interview with Inspector Roger Bartlett

QUESTIONS FOR DISCUSSION/REFLECTION

- Many churches tend to start with an answer and offer it to an area assuming they know the needs. Can you think of any examples?
- How could you research the needs of your community?
- Which partners/agencies would you consult with?
- What challenges would that bring?
- What if the social needs are bigger than the resources available?

7

GLASS HALF-FULL OR HALF-EMPTY?

Okay, I admit it, I am a glass half-full kind of person. When I hear the newsreaders telling us that the nation is in a mess I can always see their point, but my automatic pilot tells me that things will change.

I was trying to send a text message to a friend recently, asking for prayer regarding a negative comment I had received and I found that my predictive text function kept offering to complete the word I was trying to use. I got as far as the first few letters of "opposition" and the word opportunity flashed up instead! I had to stop and smile. God is so good!

When I read that the Church is in decline with the graphs showing a drop-off in attendance, and that young people are falling away in their droves, I cannot stop myself from thinking immediately about the many exceptions. It's true, many parts of the Church are in decline. But there are, at the same time, some startling stories of growth.

An international team of leading researchers based at Cranmer

Hall, Durham, has just published a study entitled *Church Growth in Britain from 1980 to the present*. Here are just a few of the extraordinary statistics that have been unearthed:

- There are 500,000 Christians in black majority churches in Britain. Sixty years ago there were hardly any.
- At least 5,000 new churches have been started in Britain since 1980 – and this is an undercount. The true figure is likely to be higher.
- There are one million Christians in Britain from black, Asian and other minority ethnic communities.
- The adult membership of the Anglican Diocese of London has risen by over 70 per cent since 1990.

As well as this, there has been growth in the number of initiatives that have been springing up to enable churches better to connect with their communities which has, in turn, led to new expressions of church.

HOPE TOGETHER [WWW.HOPETOGETHER.ORG.UK]

HOPE is a catalyst bringing churches together to transform communities. Momentum is building, including a year of mission in 2014 – the whole Church, reaching the whole nation, for a whole year. The mix of denominations, churches, ages and cultures and the number of ministries involved is unprecedented.

FRESH EXPRESSIONS [WWW.FRESHEXPRESSIONS.ORG.UK]

Fresh Expressions encourages and resources new ways of being church, working with Christians from a broad range of denominations and traditions. The movement has resulted in thousands of new congregations being formed alongside more traditional churches.

So when it comes to what we are seeing in communities across the UK with churches engaging with their community like never before, I feel optimistic about the future. I believe that this is a season of opportunity which we need to grasp.

A few years ago at our ROC launch at the Echo Arena in Liverpool, which was attended by 5,000 people, Chief Constable Matt Baggott said that we are living in days of favour and opportunity. He said there that there is a time of opportunity available to us, but he did not know how long it would last. "There are times in history when incredible things happen. I believe that this is one of those times," he added.

I think he was referring to the challenge we face in this economic crisis which has opened the door for greater collaboration between agencies partly out of necessity. The Church is well positioned to serve the community in ways which were previously closed or limited.

Far from it being a difficult time for a church or Christian organisation to grow, I believe that the opportunity before us today is the best we've ever had. So what do these opportunities look like?

MORE EFFECTIVE COMMUNITY ENGAGEMENT

Our experience in ROC has been that the demand for our work is increasing. The phone never stops ringing. Emails and invitations arrive every day seeking our advice or partnership. We currently have over 80 active enquiries from groups wanting to set up projects in partnership with us. Others are seeking our advice concerning effective engagement with public services, local authorities and other statutory bodies. The result is that we are becoming better equipped to serve our neighbourhoods in ways which make a positive impact on things like crime statistics and community wellbeing.

MORE RESOURCES ARE BEING MADE AVAILABLE

If our community work is more effective, with results to prove it, resources are released in greater measure. Many of our projects have been successful with funding bids using the ROC name and reputation. And it isn't just finance which is forthcoming, people resources – which are often hard to find – are more readily available. Volunteers are attracted to innovative projects which work. People find that by volunteering, they are able not only to make a difference but also to gain valuable experience to enhance their CV. It's a win-win situation. We have also seen buildings becoming available for our use and this is something I want to look at in more detail.

Recently I was invited to speak at Riviera Life Church in Torquay, which is part of the AOG (Assemblies of God) denomination. They are a fantastic church that offers practical support to the community in a variety of ways. As part of my trip I met with some of the other AOG Ministers from the South West. One of the questions they asked me was about community asset transfer and how it works. I shared with them the story of how we were offered our first community centre a few years ago (the Radcliffe ROC Centre featured in chapter 6) and some more recent experiences.

It occurs to me that many people will be interested in our experience and how one might look for similar opportunities in your community.

WHAT IS COMMUNITY ASSET TRANSFER?

Local authorities are empowered to transfer the ownership of land and buildings to communities for less than their market value or for a peppercorn rent. This is known as "discounted asset transfer" or "asset transfer". This shift in ownership from public bodies to communities gives greater powers to:

- Community and voluntary sector organisations.
- Community and social enterprises.
- Individuals looking to form a not-for-private-profit group to benefit their neighbourhood.

Community asset transfer can help deliver a variety of benefits but, in short, it is a key way in which local authorities can support the development of a strong, vibrant civil society through enhancing an organisation's sustainability.

Communities can enter into discussions with public bodies about Community Asset Transfer where it is their intention to promote social, economic and environmental wellbeing.

The ultimate aim of Community Asset Transfer is community empowerment – that is, to ensure that land and buildings are retained or transformed, then operated for public benefit through community asset ownership and management.

HISTORY OF COMMUNITY OWNERSHIP

The community ownership and management of assets has a history going back hundreds of years, with land and buildings promising security, wealth creation and independence. However, it is only in recent years, as the UK economy has felt the impact of deep cuts in the budgets of public bodies, that the momentum behind community asset transfer has gathered pace.

In 2007, the Government published "Making Assets Work: The Quirk Review" and went on to invest in the establishment of the Asset Transfer Unit, as well as dedicated programmes of support to affect culture change in relation to the community asset transfer agenda in England. This resulted in support for around 1,500 transfer initiatives throughout England in the period 2007-2012.

Most recently, the Government has introduced a Community Right to Bid through the Localism Act 2011. The Government aims to address concerns that too often local buildings and land that are of great value to the community, such as a village hall or local pub, go up for sale and are purchased by a private bidder before the community has the opportunity to put together the funding to take it over themselves. The Community Right to Bid gives communities the power to nominate assets (buildings or land). If the local authority agrees that the asset is of community value they will put it on a published list. If any of these assets are put up for sale, a 6-week window of opportunity is triggered, during which time any local community group may express an interest to purchase the asset. If they do express an interest, a further four and a half months window of opportunity is given so that the group may have time to find funding and put together a bid to purchase the asset on the open market.

Any voluntary or community group interested in Community Asset Transfer should consider a number of things by way of preparation:

- Check to see if your local authority has an Asset Transfer Strategy and if there have been other Community Asset Transfers nearby from which you can learn.
- Check that any land and buildings in question really are

assets and not liabilities. For example, they are liabilities if they cannot generate enough income to fund repairs, maintenance and on-going operational costs.

- Gather evidence of community support for the transfer.
- Solicit assistance or develop a business plan that demonstrates the financial viability of your plans.

Consider for a moment how many churches, organisations and charities are paying rent for the hire of a building? Add to that all those who have a building fund and who are seeking to raise funds to buy or build. Is there an opportunity for you to explore the idea of a community asset transfer?

Take a look at the following case studies, the first of which is from St Werburgh's Centre in Bristol.

CASE STUDY 1

Based in East-Central Bristol, the centre is managed by the St Werburgh's Community Association, providing facilities and meeting spaces for individuals, community groups and voluntary organisations. They run wide ranging projects for a diverse community – including Tai Chi for over 50s and cooking and gardening sessions – and they are home to over 180 member groups and five tenant organisations who are working with the local community.

The centre has been operating on this site since 1972 and in 1999 was registered as a charity and company limited by guarantee. Previously a Victorian school, St Werburgh's Centre worked closely with Bristol City Council to secure the lease. From the beginning they identified community needs – mapping and gathering opinions. The asset transfer helped them secure funding, and in June 2010 they completed a £1m Capital Project which transformed the centre into the fantastic local resource it is today. See more at: http://mycommunityrights.org.uk/case-studies/st-werburghs-centre

CASE STUDY 2

We have recently been working in Leicester following a conversation I had with the Chief Constable Simon Cole. I had tweeted Simon about our work and we subsequently arranged a phone conversation. Following that I had some meetings with some of his staff officers which resulted in two consultation events – in Loughborough and Leicester City Centre. The event in Leicester took place at a local Police station and the key leaders of some of the local city-centre churches were invited. We presented the vision and three churches were initially interested in taking the idea of partnership with us to the next stage. All three churches became ROC Partner Churches and we have subsequently been exploring different projects to suit their local context.

Trinity Life Church, led by David Hind, are exploring several projects including the ROC Family Mentoring scheme and ROC Café youth project. They were also looking for buildings around the wider Leicester area in which to plant both community projects and church. Trinity Life, like many other churches, have their own building, but they also rent other buildings as they are a multi-site church. The Police and local Council helped to facilitate a meeting which included looking at potential buildings which might be up for asset transfer and we were sent a list of 16 sites which are now being considered. Another church in the city centre, Holy Trinity, have purchased a building nearby their church and plan to open a ROC Centre there following a ROC Conversation community consultation which takes place in June 2014. The church is keen to consult with various agencies to gain a better and more detailed understanding of which needs to address. The public services and local Council have agreed not only to attend the ROC Conversation, but are also demonstrating their commitment to the whole process by including their logos in the publicity.

CASE STUDY 3

I went to visit a councillor from Wigan a few weeks ago. He had heard of our work and requested a meeting. In the course of conversation we got around to talking about community assets (okay, it's what I do now!) and he told me that 42 buildings were currently used by the Council for community services and that their work was being amalgamated into 2 buildings. The other 40 would be up for sale or asset transfer. He asked if ROC might be interested in taking one or two of these on to set up various projects which would benefit the community. And of course the answer was yes, certainly we would, but this is where we need to find a local partner church which might benefit from a building and has a vision to serve their community. My action list gets longer by the day.

The brand new ROC Centre at Launceston in Cornwall is another example of how the current economic situation has opened the way for what we still view as God's miraculous provision. When I consider the enormous challenges faced by churches over recent years to find suitable buildings and the vast fundraising efforts that have been made by leaders and members alike, I have to pinch myself to check I'm not dreaming when situations like this unfold before my very eyes. Here's the story told by John Berriman, Senior Pastor of Gateway 2 New Life Church:

"We attended the fantastic ROC Devon and Cornwall launch in October 2011 and I was very well impressed with all that ROC had achieved up until then. My wife, Sally, and I agreed to become involved in a group to take things further and soon received an invitation to meet up with others who had also responded. This coincided with our church being made aware of the possible availability of a building in our town that seemed like an ideal location, not only for our church to meet in but also maybe for a ROC Centre – the old tax office, Madford House. I went to the ROC meeting and took our newly appointed Assistant Pastor, Kevin, with me, not really knowing what we were getting into, but felt that if God was in this then we wanted in as well.

Before this meeting, what we had actually done was to have a look around the old tax office, a 10,000 sq. ft. three storey building in the heart of Launceston that had been empty for three years. They were asking a considerable amount a year to rent it – way outside our budget. As we walked around I wondered whether or not we could use such a building to hold our church meetings and also to have a ROC Centre right in the heart of Cornwall and Devon where we could perhaps have a ROC Café and many of the other successful ROC initiatives.

Those who know me know that I like to be a bit of a dealer when it comes to finances and consider myself to be quite good at negotiating (not that I won over any Dragons when I was in the Den!). I felt that it was right to offer them 10% of what they are asking per year. The representative of the company said that he would have to put the offer to his client and I naturally thought that they might say no and at least try to negotiate upwards. Clearly God had other plans because they didn't – they came back and said that they would accept our offer and wanted us to proceed as soon as possible. To me this did not seem quite right. In my mind that was too easy and so we made a few enquiries and found out that whoever took on the building was going to have a possible £25,000 dilapidation order placed upon them!

After more negotiations we finally settled on an amazing figure that will allow us to develop a community centre in the heart of Launceston, which will not hinder us as a growing church and will also allow us to undertake community projects fairly quickly. Our vision has kept us going over the past 13 months while the paperwork was going through. If anything, this time has helped us to develop an idea of how to create a ROC Community Hub and to seek God's will on the building as a whole. It is one thing looking at taking on a large building, but it is another thing when you hold the keys and think, 'Where do we start?'

We found ourselves very much outside our comfort zones in May 2013 when we decided to hold a ROC Conversation. At that point we had only been in Launceston for three years and now we were going out to the community and asking them what they felt could be better in our town. Although the invites went out and follow-up calls were made, we weren't sure how many would turn up, if any. How big is our faith you might ask? Well over 60 people turned up from different agencies and we had a great evening talking about our town. It has to be said that ROC has really helped us open doors to get into the wider community – from sitting in Police stations drinking tea with the local Beat Manager to visiting day centres to explore ways in which we can help, none of this would have taken place without the support of ROC. I even had a phone call from a senior manager within Cornwall Council one evening at 9pm during a small group meeting to find out more about what we were up to – but that's another story. Back to the vision: being a pioneer is what I am all about and being a pioneer for ROC in Cornwall excites me.

Looking back at the journey we have been on over the past 12 months is incredible. Setting up Cornwall's first ROC Hub will see us using just over half of the ground floor with a purpose built serving area as well as a pool table, games console and other elements that would keep young people in a safe environment. [As I write this I have recently heard that the youth centre in Launceston is to close for budget reasons, so the timing seems great for a ROC Café to open]. I see a vision for there to be community groups set up to look at issues of unemployment, wellbeing, vulnerability, youth and young families. The opportunities seem endless, but we realise that God is in control.

We have many ideas for other parts of the building and the challenge is to know just what the right projects are. In February 2014, some 13 months after our meeting in Exeter, we held our first ROC (Cornwall and Devon) meeting in our NEW (still being refurbished) Gateway Centre (with proper Cornish pasties for lunch!) and we are very excited not only that our church fellowship will meet there, but that it will be an excellent centre for ROC in the heart of Cornwall and Devon working alongside the Police and Fire services and trying to fully resource unmet social needs within the community of Launceston. If I had the chance to do it all again, would I? Too right I would!"

So it's a glass half-full for me. That doesn't mean we never wobble in the face of many significant challenges that come our way, but we do set ourselves positively and seek to make the most of every opportunity. If we look with eyes of faith we can see the potential to grow. Even some of the things which were previously viewed as barriers or obstacles can be seen in a new light. The main thing is to have a clear vision of what you want to achieve and to look for the doors which might be opening – perhaps doors you haven't noticed before.

ROC Conversation Launceston

QUESTIONS FOR DISCUSSION/REFLECTION

- Does your natural personality fit best with a glass half full or empty mind set? What are the dangers of each approach?
- How can I and my church make the most of opportunities to serve my community?
- Am I actively looking for opportunities?
- Do I see the problem and feel overwhelmed or can I see the potential solution?
- Would my church or project benefit from the use of a building?
- What preparation would we need to make to take advantage of an asset transfer?

8 WHAT'S IN A NAME?

A few years ago I was flicking through a Christian magazine when I noticed an advertisement for something new: Spring Harvest Holidays in France. The Spring Harvest logo was what initially caught my attention, that pair of orange and green stick people with outstretched arms, looking as though they're suspended in mid air by invisible wires. I didn't have to read any of the copy in the ad because, within a split second, I got the message. What a great idea: a combination of excellent Bible teaching, worship times, groups for the kids and, instead of the bracing weather of Skegness or Minehead, a week of decent sunshine on the famous Vendée, the beautiful coastal strip on the Western edge of France.

Spring Harvest began life in Easter 1979 at a cold, damp holiday camp in North Wales. Around 2,700 Christians from varying church backgrounds attended a week of "modern-style worship", Bible teaching and workshops about the relevance of Christian faith to everyday life. The event has taken place every year since during the Easter holidays. Frank and I have been involved in almost every one and our four children have catalogues of positive memories of many special times when they met with God and made new friends.

35 years on, guests are hosted in modern Butlins holiday resorts with luxury (warm) chalet accommodation, hi-tech entertainment venues, ultramodern water worlds and a huge range of leisure facilities. The largest worship gatherings welcome over 3,000 people who still come from every church background across the UK and beyond. The learning together still focuses on applying the Christian faith to the challenges and realities of life. The entertainment ranges from Butlins free fairground to late night stand up comedy and music acts.

Spring Harvest attendance over the past 35 years has totalled over one million people. Over ten million pounds has been raised for charitable projects around the world. Over 100 music albums have introduced new worship songs, children's resources and live worship to a wider audience.

Now, the purpose of this chapter is not to persuade you to book a Spring Harvest holiday in either France or the UK – although you wouldn't be disappointed if you did – what I want to talk about is how valuable a recognised name can be, especially when that name has grown in stature and reputation over the years through delivering high quality service, keeping its promises, holding fast to its core principles and achieving impressive outcomes.

There are those in some Christian circles who would be critical of the idea of an organisation, ministry or church becoming "well known" in the sense of having a clear brand. I'm not sure if this is something to do with our British culture or not, but there does seem to be a school of thought that suggests there is something wrong with doing well and earning a reputation that creates a prominent, high-profile image.

Thankfully, this way of thinking hasn't hindered organisations like Alpha, which has become the world's most effective course for introducing people to Christianity. Alpha began life in 1977 as an in-house, basic Christianity course for members of Holy Trinity Church of England in Brompton, London. By the way, let's give credit here to Rev Charles Marnham who created it and his wife, Tricia, who came up with the name. It started to become well known from around 1990 when then curate Nicky Gumbel revised and updated it and made it available to other churches. To date around 40,000 courses have been run in 169 countries by a wide range of churches, with in excess of 18 million people attending, 2.5 million of those in the UK.

Amazing, isn't it? And yet, run a Google search for "Alpha Course" and the fourth ranking site is one disparaging and attacking the course under the heading "Dangers of the Alpha Course", posted by a group of (hopefully) well-meaning Christians. You can't please everyone.

The point is, there can be real value in earning a deserved reputation that leads to the name of an organisation becoming quickly recognisable. Spring Harvest are not claiming to be better than other Christian holidays. Neither are they trying to say there is anything inferior about alternative Bible weeks. All that has happened is that their name has become synonymous with a trustworthy product.

Similarly, Alpha do not set themselves up as being the only way to find out how to become a Christian. It's just that, over the last twenty years people have had great experiences of

Alpha and talked about it so much that the name has become prominent.

Similar observations can be made about many other Christian organisations and churches. Willow Creek Church in Chicago, Saddleback Church in California, Oasis, Street Pastors, Christians Against Poverty (CAP) and many other worthy ministries ... their names have become renowned because of the quality and scale of their excellent work.

Recently, I was sitting in a Costa Coffee outlet in a large city centre with a group of Christians and the subject of well-known Christian initiatives came up for discussion. There was a lively and healthy debate about the value of using recognised Christian "brands" to promote the ideals of unity and community transformation. Some were uncomfortable with the whole thing and felt it was in some way not particularly "spiritual". The general consensus, however, was positive and we came to a reasonable level of agreement that as long as the "label" being used had genuine substance and a broad degree of support across a wide range of groupings, then it could only be a good thing. The overriding view was that a reputation could only be properly earned over time and it would be unwise to try to make use of a new or unproven name to try to garner support for a multi-agency venture.

I'm sure it had escaped the notice of some of the group that we were having this discussion in a Costa Coffee outlet! Which got me thinking about the recent explosion of High Street coffee shops. It wasn't that long ago that the must-have-drink to be seen carrying to work in the morning was a bottle of water. Now it's a takeaway Starbucks cup. Or should it be Costa?

As a tea drinker, I don't have much of a view about which

coffee franchise to visit. The tea tastes the same in all of them and the differences in décor and ambiance are neither here nor there for me. I have friends, however, who have a definite pecking order in their minds and they will drive past one well-known store in the hope that their favourite is nearby. There must be all kinds of subtle influences involved in this: the finer points of which beans are grown where; what grinding process is used by one company in comparison with the competition; how the drinks are sized and priced and so on. But it's all wasted on those of us who are not interested in coffee. The value of the coffee shop phenomenon to me is that it provides a useful place to meet. We used to have meetings in burger stores, which was not pleasant with sometimes noisy groups of schoolchildren, the unhealthy aroma of cooking fat and uncomfortable hard plastic seats. Nero's is much better. Or is it Coffee Republic?

As I mull over the debate about the value of Christian "brands" I begin to realise that we're not comparing like with like. Commercial branding, marketing, advertising and franchising are all to do with competition. Each company is trying to find an edge over its rivals in order to maximise profits. Staying with coffee shops for the moment, all the players would agree that they have one huge core philosophy very much in common: freshly brewed coffee. Their differences, such as where they source their beans and how they grind them, what type of food items they sell in addition, the style of the furnishings, the music, the uniforms and the myriad other minor variants, are very much secondary. Their collective mission is to convert instant coffee drinkers to the real thing and keep them coming back. How they carve up the market is certainly of real interest to the shareholders, but they are all essentially in the same business.

As consumers, we are confronted with the branding battles that occur on our high streets (and increasingly online) as rivals in various sectors jockey for pole position in our attentions. We regularly hear about the Big Four Banks and the Big Four supermarkets (or is it five now?) and the news is always to do with how they compare against each other.

When we talk about Christian "branding" however, we are not in competition with each other for market share and here is the big difference. If a Christian ministry becomes a "household name" because it does something especially well, then where is the problem with it enjoying the benefits of branding?

There are alternative courses available for people to discover what Christianity is all about. One example is Christianity Explored, which has been developed over ten years by All Souls Church, Langham Place in London. The course has a distinctive theological emphasis which differs from Alpha in a number of ways and, rather than being viewed as a competitor in "the market", can be seen quite clearly as a strong brand in its own right, representing a particular expression of Christianity.

To use a different example, many churches have started their own debt counselling services, which help a lot of people. Could they do a better job by linking up with CAP, rather than owning it themselves? Undoubtedly, simply because CAP's name has become well known in the finance industry and they are very highly thought of by banks and credit companies. CAP helps its clients to negotiate fair repayment plans and to achieve their financial targets. Therefore, when a CAP representative calls a credit card company on behalf of someone drowning in debt, the company is generally keen to agree a solution that throws the client a lifeline. Thanks to the CAP brand, thousands of people are finding ways of stabilising their finances and discovering in the process there's a God who loves them enough to provide them with volunteers who will support them.

WHY REINVENT THE WHEEL?

One of the main reasons for linking up with an established and trusted brand, either as a commercial franchisee or a partner in a spiritual initiative, is the fact that a lot of the hard work has already been done. A concept has been thought-through, researched and developed, tried and tested, reviewed and refined, reviewed again and improved. Time, energy and money has been expended in the process to date and there is a reservoir of intellectual and emotional capital on hand.

To "reinvent the wheel" is to duplicate a basic method that has already previously been created or optimised by others. The inspiration for this idiomatic metaphor lies in the fact that the wheel is the archetype of human ingenuity, both by virtue of the added power and flexibility it affords its users, and also in the ancient origins which allow it to underlie much, if not all, of modern technology.

Since it has already been invented, and is not considered to have any operational flaws, an attempt to reinvent it would be pointless and add no value to the object. It would be a waste of time, diverting resources from other possibly more worthy goals through which our skills could advance more substantially.

The challenge then, is to learn from others and build on the success of proven models. We need to put aside any pride and link up with others who are a few pages ahead. Good things deserve to be replicated for the greater good of more communities.

Without ever setting out to impress anyone, ROC has

established a reputation among secular agencies as a trustworthy and effective broker of partnerships that gets things done in local communities. Everyone knows that ROC is a Christian charity and yet, despite the strong philosophy of political correctness that pervades the public sector, we are welcomed, valued and appreciated by Chiefs of Police, Government officials both locally and nationally, business leaders and Chief Executives of many other agencies. We are also highly regarded by senior Church leaders across the various denominations.

This means that churches all over the UK with a vision for community action projects, who understand the value of forming partnerships with other like-minded local groups, can use our name to gain access to high level decision makers who would otherwise be less than enthusiastic about any sort of conversation. Many agencies are simply unable to link directly with a church or any other faith-based group whose aims are overtly religious. Legally binding constitutions prevent partnerships of this sort. Similarly, many funding bodies are restricted legally in their ability to make grants to religious groups. There are, of course, some notable exceptions. Some grant-making trusts can only give to religious activities. The point is that if a church sets up a ROC project it can enjoy the best of both worlds. While on the subject of funding, it's also worth noting that many donor bodies can only support projects that are very localised, even to the smallest geographical area in some cases. Here again, a ROC partner church can benefit from both aspects: the ROC name, which is nationally recognised as credible and worthy, and the specific locality of the project, which matches the unique criterion of the Trust.

Across the ROC network there many ideas being shared,

borrowed and directly copied. The unique ROC Café, for example, is a model that has lent itself to both replication and modification according to location and need. There are ROC Cafés for teenagers, for pre-teens and even younger children. What they all have in common is that they involve a number of different agencies in their delivery. Most will have some traditional elements, such as pool and table tennis but, in all probability, there won't be any two that are identical in the range of activities on offer.

One great idea that was suggested to us a year or so ago, and is now well established, is the ROC Café Bus aimed at older people. Again, this has proven to be an excellent combination of the ROC name combining with local vision and energy in a pioneering project which is inspiring others nearby to consider replicating it for themselves. The principal visionary and project leader is Marian Ayres from Littlehampton in Sussex. Here's the story behind how she saw a need in her community and how God used her to make it a reality.

"Littlehampton, the little family holiday resort on the sunny south coast, has an estate called 'Wick'. There are some amazing people who live there, but it also has all the deprivation and child poverty labels. As the Town Councillor for that Ward I want to see the downward trends reversed.

We have a large number of over sixty-five year olds living alone due to the loss of a partner and fear of crime and ill health has led to a lot of loneliness and isolation.

So, supported by two wonderful trust funds and a variety of agencies – Police, churches, councils and a number of lovely volunteers who want to see the community transformed – we amassed over £12,000 and bought a mobile community centre. Our ROC Café Bus is a three quarter length converted single decker which we located through 'Working on Wheels' (formerly the National Playbus). It can hold around fifteen people comfortably for light refreshments – tea, coffee and cake or cream teas (or should that be veggie dips!) – and sitting down activities.

We park for two hour sessions in ten suitable roads every week for continuity and building relationships. Older folk can meet their neighbours and be a part of the community. The bus is for everyone who is around during the day, so intergenerational friendships can be formed and neighbourly care develop whether it's through garden produce sharing, giving parenting advice and support or just having the opportunity to feel accepted and valued.

The Police and Community Support Officers (PCSO's) 'pop-in' to meet and listen to residents and to allay fears, although I suspect the cream teas hold some attraction! Other organisations like Age UK's Health and Wellbeing teams have offered to join up with us and share their expertise. The team of key volunteers have been recruited mainly from those at the ROC launch and the ROC Conversation community consultation in Littlehampton last winter.

We want to balance 'best practice' and common sense and make this a truly community-run facility, recognising the gifts and expertise often lying dormant for the want of an initiative that is near at hand and not too demanding on time. Each Café stop will work independently within the aims and objectives of our constitution, diversifying according to the needs identified. When talking to residents, about seventy per cent have expressed enthusiasm to meet with us. We want to have times of caring and sharing, but inject a bit of fun into what is often the only outing in their week.

Backing us are teams of lovely people who want to do practical jobs for people to make their lives easier. Representatives from local clubs and activity groups will come aboard to encourage further links into the town and church resources.

We cannot wait to see how this God-inspired, prayer-backed project develops. 'Wick's got Talent' isn't just for the younger people."

What a great project! I am inspired by people like Marian. She is responding to a need and using her talents to make a difference. She had to step out in faith at the beginning of the project with no way of knowing whether her idea would work.

Her story doesn't end there though, as others inspired by what she is doing are now following in her footsteps with the ROC Bus idea which is being replicated in other areas.

The Police and Crime Commissioner of Sussex, Katy Bourne, has recently been to visit the ROC Bus and has sent us a warm message of her support as well as some tweets. In another part of the county Paul Wilson has been pioneering another new ROC project – ROC Family mentoring, which has started in Arun. Projects like these can easily be replicated in other areas and we are so grateful for this pioneering work.

QUESTIONS FOR DISCUSSION/REFLECTION

- Why are brands like CAP, Alpha and Street Pastors successful?
- Why are we sometimes resistant to the idea of "branding" when it comes to Christians initiatives?
- Are you aware of any great ideas which have not been replicated?
- Why is it sometimes better to use a tested model rather than starting up something new yourself?
- What are the challenges to using an existing brand? I.e. cost
- Do brands impose too many conditions?
- How can we share best practice and reach more communities?

Interview with Marian Ayres – ROC Bus

9
STEP-BY-STEP GUIDE

Recent conversations have convinced me that this chapter is a must. People often ask us, "How do we actually start a project?" What are the steps? Where do we begin?

At a recent meeting with church leaders, when it was mentioned that I had written two books (City-Changing Prayer in 2005 and Redeeming Our Communities in 2008) one of the leaders said, "I will buy both the books and I expect they will tell me how ROC works."

"Actually, they don't," I thought. The other books are much more about the philosophy and foundations of what we do now and were written before we even started community based projects. So this is a very practical chapter outlining the steps to setting up effective and sustainable projects.

Let's start with a straightforward and simple question: What makes something a ROC project? A ROC project can be almost anything which meets a community need, from tackling anti-social behaviour amongst young people, through the pressures experienced by many families, to the isolation and loneliness faced by many elderly people. ROC has a model for each of these. The list of our project ideas is always growing and some are at a more advanced stage of evolution than others. Here are some examples:

ROC CAFÉ

Our most highly-developed project to date. A ROC Café is a multi-agency supported youth drop-in project which provides healthy diversionary activities for young people. This project works well in areas where there are insufficient activities for young people or that has significant reports of anti-social behaviour. The most obvious locations for a ROC Café are areas of high social deprivation, but the model is equally valued in more settled suburban settings. Young people at every level of society are suffering from many issues that can be addressed well through the ROC Café model.

ROC CARE

This aims to improve the quality of life for elderly people by providing visitors who call at the person's home by appointment, mainly just to chat. The number of older people who tell us that they hardly ever have a meaningful conversation from one week to the next is quite startling. ROC Care projects also organise social activities to provide opportunities for peer friendships. These may be tea dances, lunches, bingo and so on. Some are regular, weekly activities; others occasional. One innovative idea I have just heard about is a group that has applied to a local trust for a grant to buy a number of Kindle devices to lend their members to help acquaint them with the world of technology at an accessible level.

Some ROC Care projects find ways of teaming up with groups that provide volunteers to help with odd jobs around the house. A ROC Care initiative in Stockport teamed up with a local social enterprise to do a garden makeover for a 92 year old local lady. Ann Russell, who leads ROC Care in Stockport, had been visiting Margaret for a few months. Through her visits Ann found that Margaret's garden was in severe need of tidying up. In fact, Ann discovered that Margaret had been living with her curtains drawn for over 17 years because she didn't want to see the state of her garden.

The team did a great job of clearing out the garden, laying down some bark and re-setting the paving stones. Neighbours from across the road also donated shrubs and flowers. Margaret was thrilled with the results and told us, "People have commented on the garden saying it's beautiful and I think so too. I look forward to opening my curtains every morning now!"

Becky from the ROC office also volunteered to help out and said, "It's amazing to see how volunteering a small amount of time and energy can have a huge impact on somebody's life." Dominic Mould, the manager of the Social Enterprise that provided the volunteer labour, commented that it was a great project for his lads to be involved with: "It's put a spring in their step knowing they've made a difference – they are ex-offenders who have become Christians in prison and nothing gives them greater pleasure than knowing they have brought some blessing to someone through the work of their hands."

ROC MENTORS

This initiative seeks to provide an early intervention mentoring scheme, primarily for young people aged 13-17 years, who will be referred either by the Police or Youth Offending Service.

Many of the young people who could benefit from mentoring come from chaotic family backgrounds, often where there is an absence of good male role models able to exert a positive influence on them as they grow up. However, the problem, whilst predominantly about young males is certainly not exclusive to males. We are seeing increasing numbers of young females coming to the notice of police and criminal justice agencies. Whilst overall figures remain low compared to males, the number of arrests of females for violent offences has doubled over the last decade.

ROC RESTORE

This is a form of restorative justice undertaken by community members in facilitated meetings. The aim is to bring together the victims and perpetrators of low level crime, anti-social behaviour and nuisance in a meeting where trained volunteers use restorative or reparative approaches to agree on a course of action for those involved. There is a detailed explanation of the subject of restorative justice in the following chapter.

ROC ADVICE

A service which offers a variety of support and advice for a wide range of issues including housing, domestic violence and family-related issues.

ROC Advice is a new project that has been pioneered by the community in Eastbourne. In the absence of the Citizens Advice

Bureau, which had been shut down, the Eastbourne Christian Agencies Network felt very strongly that there was a great need in the town centre for a hub where various agencies, faith-based and secular, could supply help on issues like benefits and tribunal hearings, employment and housing matters and provide counselling for both families and children.

Within a short time the YMCA agreed that the facility they had in the town centre, which had been dormant for some years, could be rented at a much reduced cost for a period of one year. In May 2011 the centre opened at 95 Seaside Road, housing a benefit and counselling service on Mondays and Thursdays, a children's and family support service on Tuesdays, employment support on Wednesdays, life skills on Fridays and learning English on Saturdays. 400 people used the centre in the first 2 weeks of it opening. ROC Advice provides a successful model which can be replicated in other communities with similar needs across the UK.

ROC CENTRE

A multi-agency led community centre which provides multiple activities and a safe meeting place for people of all ages in a community. There is a detailed explanation with examples in chapter 5.

GETTING INVOLVED

STEP ONE...

...is to become a Partner Church (or Organisation).

A ROC Partner Church/Organisation is, first of all, a supporter of our national work. We ask that Partners raise our profile within their own networks by regularly circulating news and prayer points, encouraging people to receive our prayer bulletins and to consider becoming personal supporters of ROC. Our budget is growing faster than our income due to ever-increasing demand for our services.

Partner Churches/Organisations agree to demonstrate their support by giving either a monthly gift of at least £25 as a token of their partnership in the Gospel or an annual gift raised through an offering on ROC Sunday – a day where our work is featured prominently in the services. In some cases we can supply a team member to attend and preach if requested sufficiently in advance. Some churches give both a monthly gift and take up an annual offering.

STEP TWO...

...is to suggest a project to be launched in partnership. The Partner Church/Organisation contacts ROC HQ to discuss the project proposal. There is checklist of criteria that need to be present before a project can be considered. The list includes: suitable premises; a credible, experienced project leader; availability of a team of volunteers; some warm contacts with other local agencies. If not all the criteria are in place ROC may be able to help. Sometimes it can take months to get all the criteria in place, but it's worth taking the time to do so. An effective, sustainable project requires solid foundations and strong multi-agency relationships – neither of which can be rushed.

STEP THREE...

...is to hold a ROC Conversation (see chapter 6). ROC will provide the majority of the organisational work for this as well as inviting other agencies. A ROC team will visit and facilitate the Conversation in partnership with the local leadership. There is a cost associated with this which is usually met by a local funding source.

STEP FOUR...

...is to recruit a local enabling group, set targets, raise profile locally and raise funds – all of this with plenty of support from ROC National (see the story about the ROC Parkhead enabling group in chapter 6).

STEP FIVE...

...and beyond is to develop and expand through a process of continual review and evaluation in conjunction with ROC National. Most ROC projects evolve uniquely to meet their own specific local needs, but they do so as part of the national network, learning from and supporting one another.

FAQs

Q1 Why use the ROC banner?

This is a question that is often in the minds of people we meet, but it's seldom clearly articulated. A few years ago if I was asked this question I would have said that the principle was the important thing, not the name. It was good enough just to see the work being done or at least attempted. Now I would answer differently. I have to say that our name is vital because of the strong reputation ROC has earned over these last ten years, particularly among senior leaders of public service organisations. Here is a brief summary of the benefits:

- **Name awareness** – when setting up a project and seeking support, the ROC name increases credibility. Because it is nationally recognised and respected it opens doors at the highest levels within Police forces, Fire and Rescue services and local authorities.
- **Dedicated support** – a ROC Project Manager is assigned to your project to provide individual advice, support and access to resources.
- **National network** – ROC Projects and Partners are available for consultation and discussion.
- **Highly developed resources** – online access is provided to project ideas, practical tools, funding advice and much more.
- **Branding** – a range of professional publicity and promotional materials is available and your project will be highlighted on our national website.
- **Fundraising** – ROC has proved a successful umbrella for sourcing funding that is not always accessible directly by churches.
- **Training opportunities** – access to online tutorials and local workshops.

Q2 Why is there a minimum donation of £25 per month to ROC National?

This amount, often covered by a ROC Partner Church, is a token of support and partnership in the Gospel. It demonstrates tangibly a joining of heart and spirit and lays the foundation for a potential project partnership, subject to all the relevant criteria being in place. It contributes to the cost of Head Office support, both in the setup stage and in providing on going support of the project post-launch.

This includes not only personal support via telephone and email but also access to a wide range of materials to help each project succeed i.e. funding advice, policies, promotional materials, artwork for publicity and much more.

Q3 Where does the project funding come from?

Funding for existing ROC projects comes from a variety of sources: grant making trusts, local businesses, individual and church donations, public services and fundraising events. In our experience, ROC projects find it relatively easy to raise the funds for local projects since the amounts required are not huge and local vision is often strong. Many local trusts are only able to give to very localised work, which means they often have surplus funds and are not resistant to applications.

ROC HQ provides invaluable support in applying for funds and, where relevant, a small percentage of the funds raised by each local project goes towards ROC HQ central costs. A service level agreement explains all this in detail.

Q4 Where can you access crime stats and local social needs?

We recommend that you carefully evidence the need for a ROC

Centre as a key element of your case. This is essential for gaining the commitment and support of partners for the project. Evidence in the form of crime and anti-social behaviour statistics can be obtained from the local Police and your Council's planning team. Most police websites publish local crime statistics.

ROC advises holding a ROC Conversation consultation event prior to opening the ROC Centre as outlined in chapter 6. This open-invitation community meeting allows all partners, along with the local community, to discuss the needs of the community and how the ROC Centre will contribute to its wellbeing.

How do you find out who your local Police Service and Fire and Rescue contacts are? Visit your local Police Service or Fire and Rescue websites. ROC HQ can also introduce you to key contacts because of our good standing and relations with public services and statutory authorities.

Q5 What does ROC provide in terms of on-going support?

The ROC National office provides advice and expertise at each stage of the process. We provide publicity design, social media marketing, fundraising advice and contacts, training workshops and contacts with public services. The growing network of ROC Projects is also accessible through the ROC head office.

Q6 Is faith promoted at a ROC project or ROC Centre?

The simple answer is no. ROC projects/centres do not promote faith. Many of the volunteers have a faith, but find that their actions speak louder than words.

ROC projects are Christian-led and provide opportunities for Christian volunteers to build bridges for the Gospel by developing relationships with not-yet-Christians and demonstrating the love and reality of God in practical action.

Q7 What happens at a ROC Centre?

Each centre has the flexibility to design its own activities and projects based on the needs of the community and resources available. A typical centre might include a ROC Café, mums and tots playgroup, homework clubs, advice sessions, family mentoring, drop-in sessions for different target groups and so on. There could be provision for existing non-ROC branded projects which can help contribute towards the running costs of a centre. Preference for these projects is given to the partner agencies and organisations on the management committee.

Q8 Who runs the ROC Centre?

Part of the DNA of a ROC Centre is the necessity of a multi-agency approach. We encourage consultation between the agencies from the very beginning of the process. Ideal partners include Fire and Rescue, Police Service, local authority, local churches, residents' groups, housing associations and high schools. These organisations can help to identify the social needs faced by your community and how the ROC Centre can seek to address some of these needs. It is suggested that a small team is appointed with a representative from each or most of these agencies to oversee the project. The local management team/enabling group has a strong link with the ROC HQ staff team and is part of a national vision.

Q9 What is the timescale required for setting up a ROC Centre?

This can be anything from 6 weeks to 6 months. Timings depend on finding a suitable building and getting the right team in place or amalgamating projects that are already established. Thought needs to be given to recruiting the right volunteers and ensuring DBS checks are completed.

Q10 How much does it cost to set up and run a ROC Centre?

Costs depend on the condition of the building you are proposing to use and based on the building being free of charge (rent and utilities). Running costs once the centre has been set up are minimal, but may include the purchase of new equipment, the replacement of old equipment and the costs of utilities, activity materials (crafts) and repairs. All of these are based on the premise that the ROC Centre is run primarily by volunteers.

Q11 What age group is the ROC Centre aimed at?

A ROC Centre is purposed to support the whole community, from young to elders, with a strong emphasis on intergenerational activities. This needs to be considered when deciding on the activities and projects to be held at the centre, so there is not an overemphasis on one age group over another – unless the local community decides it is most appropriate for the area.

Q12 What sort of building or venue is most suitable to accommodate a ROC Centre?

A ROC Centre is ideally situated in a building dedicated for its use. With careful planning it could be run through other venues, although this may limit the opportunities for projects as a result. The ideal location should be in reasonable condition to begin with. It is best to have a working kitchen, a large hall, two or three break out rooms, a small office area and storage space.

The location is a major consideration. A ROC Centre is best placed in an accessible area where the community is likely to gather. The Police and local Council are usually very helpful in identifying suitable buildings and locations for the ROC Café.

10 THE LESSON OF THE LOAVES

As we come towards the end of the book I want to return to the lesson of the loaves. It's about trusting Jesus, but it's more about learning how we can cooperate with the Holy Spirit and participate in the miracles of God.

Learning is the essence of discipleship. The New Testament Greek word for disciple or Christ-follower is mathētēs, which simply means "learner". Plenty of sermons have used the illustration of Christians wearing L-Plates as a sign of their status as spiritual trainees, but there is a flaw in the car-driving analogy – real L-Plates are always temporary. Eventually one of two things will happen: the learner will graduate and immediately become recognised as an expert (!) or, after countless failed attempts to pass the test, he or she will admit defeat and return to public transport. In either case the L-Plates are discarded.

A better term, which is now broadly used in educational circles, is that of Life-long Learning – first coined in the 1920s by an academic called Basil Yeaxlee to provide an intellectual basis for a comprehensive understanding of education as a continuing aspect of everyday life. Further Education Colleges now refer to their sphere of activity as The Life Long Learning Sector. It's fine as a definition, but in reality most students probably still discard their "L-Plates" when they gain their qualification.

Life-long learning is, nevertheless, a perfect description of what it means to follow Jesus. He used the term disciple to describe those who followed him and it's clear that he expected them (and us) to start learning from day one and to continue to grow in the understanding of God and his Kingdom.

At the beginning of this book we looked at the miracle of the feeding of the five thousand recorded in all four Gospels, the thrust of which was that Jesus expected his disciples to learn that they could and should participate with him in meeting the needs of the crowds.

Remember, when they observed the need and came to him he replied, "You feed them." Surely this was not possible. They had neither access to food nor the cash to buy it. The master wasn't convinced by their argument. He knew what was possible and he wanted his students to learn something important about laying hold of that. When the solitary lunch was offered he helped with the first stage of the miracle, blessing and breaking the bread and fish, but he didn't let the learners off the hook. He gave the pieces to his disciples and instructed them to distribute them. As they obeyed, the miracle occurred, right there in front of their eyes. One by one the hungry people were fed and the food just kept on coming.

And to underline the learning, there was a visual aid: twelve full baskets of leftovers.

Lesson summary: when you're faced with a challenge, no matter how huge, trust God. But don't forget that he trusts you and wants you to get involved in his miracles. You always have a part to play. So go for it with whatever you have available. He will do the rest.

For whatever reason, however, these disciples were not able to understand the point. Perhaps they were simply awestruck – after all, it was a stunning miracle. Maybe they learned only part of the lesson: that Jesus is able to do miracles. They clearly did not grasp the fact that they were expected to play their part, hence the summary point at the end of the next piece of narrative recorded in Mark 6: 45-52:

"Immediately Jesus made his disciples get into the boat and go on ahead of him to Bethsaida, while he dismissed the crowd. After leaving them, he went up on a mountainside to pray Later that night, the boat was in the middle of the lake, and he was alone on land. He saw the disciples straining at the oars, because the wind was against them. Shortly before dawn he went out to them, walking on the lake. He was about to pass by them, but when they saw him walking on the lake, they thought he was a ghost. They cried out, because they all saw him and were terrified. Immediately he spoke to them and said, 'Take courage! It is I. Don't be afraid.' Then he climbed into the boat with them, and the wind died down. They were completely amazed, for **they had not understood about the loaves**; their hearts were hardened."

This is the story of what followed the miracle of the loaves. The disciples enter into a boat to cross over to the city of Bethsaida. Jesus was going to meet them there. When out in the lake, a storm arose that threatened to capsize their boat and endanger their lives. Fear and anxiety gripped the disciples' hearts and they began to panic in the throes of the strong wind and waves.

Notice verse 52. Mark points out something which happened earlier that afternoon that should have helped them that night on the sea. In the KJV verse 52 reads, "They considered not the miracle of the loaves." I strongly suggest that in the feeding of the five thousand, Jesus was teaching them something that would be a help to them in the midst of life's storms.

When Jesus performed this miracle it was not for show. Nor was he performing to impress the disciples. Primarily it was to meet the needs of the hungry people, but he was also teaching his friends. They were being given a lesson in God's School of Higher Learning.

This situation is different. This time they face a storm, but the lesson is the same. You can almost hear Jesus say, "*You* calm the storm."

When it comes to feeding a crowd with very little food or calming an angry storm, we need to learn the same lesson. It's a situation which requires greater faith. Faith which has been stretched before. Lessons already learned about how God's Kingdom advances should produce a greater willingness in our hearts to trust him and cooperate.

Hopefully, as you've read about the life-changing work going on through networks of ordinary people in ROC projects across the UK you'll have seen the common theme: Christians trusting God, noticing need, looking at available resources and going for it in faith, believing that he will do the rest.

In John 14:12 Jesus urges his learners to put their faith in him to the extent that, even once he has left their physical presence they will be equipped by the Holy Spirit to co-work with God in demonstrations of the Kingdom that meet people's needs, sometimes in amazing ways: "Truly, truly, I say to you, he who believes in Me, the works that I do, he will do also; and greater works than these he will do; because I go to the Father."

There are many ways of interpreting this, including references to miracles in Acts where people were healed miraculously through touching an Apostle's handkerchief; the Gospel proclaimed to thousands simultaneously in a miracle of linguistic communication. Others point to the planting of churches worldwide and the enormous numerical growth of the Christian family. We should also consider the many amazing medical and scientific breakthroughs enabled by believers through the centuries and the countless social reforms that have improved life for people all over the world.

In the two thousand years since the first coming of Christ on the earth society has radically changed, but the needs are arguably greater today than ever before. Which means there are still plenty of opportunities for more "greater things" to be done in partnership with him and through the leading of his Spirit.

The prayer Jesus taught us to pray includes the phrase, "Let your Kingdom come on earth as it is in heaven". It really strikes a chord when it comes to seeing his activity unfold in our lives. We pray and learn to "be the answer". In this we are discovering his will for our communities and we become part of the solution.

Every situation is different, but we have the same opportunity to learn and respond. I love the phrase "life-long learning" because there is always so much more to discover. The older we get the more opportunity we have to learn.

In the 1990s, seemingly out of nowhere, the WWJD wristband suddenly appeared. Almost overnight Christian young people were sporting a new fashion accessory – one that carried a compelling idea. The challenge was, when faced with a moral or ethical issue, to ask the question: What Would Jesus Do? Great as this is in terms of keeping Jesus and his Kingdom central to our thinking, it only does part of the job doesn't it? We can answer the question in theory, in silence, in a doctrinally accurate manner and still actually do nothing at all. This is a recurring problem in Christian circles. We sometimes become so preoccupied with a set of beliefs that we forget they are supposed to affect the way we act. My friend, Malcolm Duncan, wrote this in the 2014 Spring Harvest Theme Guide: "Believing as a way of life that shapes your attitudes, your actions and your character."

For example, you see a beggar sitting on the ground outside the coffee shop and you ask yourself, What Would Jesus Do? There is no right answer by the way, apart from, "Whatever he saw the Father doing" or "Whatever the Spirit led him to do". To suggest that Jesus had a standard way of responding to people in certain circumstances would be wrong. Unless, maybe, we could say, "He would view the person with compassion…"

You can see where this kind of theorising takes us. On the plus side it's great that we're asking the question, but we do need to respond actively and actually do something.

In this case we can always pray quickly for the beggar, ask the Spirit to direct us if there is something specific we should do, listen for the prompting and act. Perhaps stooping for a quick chat to acknowledge the person's humanity? Maybe offering to buy some food? More often than not we're in such a hurry that we can't do more than pray a quick prayer or just smile and make eye contact. Perhaps the Spirit may tell us not to be in such a hurry so often.

On a larger scale, when we start to observe the needs of our community, of course we must ask God what is needed. The lesson of the loaves tells us that our own personal involvement, limited though it may be, is a vital piece of the picture. You feed them. You speak to the storm. As James writes in his epistle, faith without deeds is dead.

What I have learned over the years is that we need to ask the Lord to show us how to begin to respond to a need and then have the courage to follow his prompting – not just asking but also following. Each time we choose this path we grow in our understanding and our experience of his power.

Thank God for a great many agencies who are making massive strides forwards with humanitarian efforts to meet many of the world's pressing needs. Most, if not all of these began in a very small way: one or two people observing a need, stepping out in faith to do the little they could and trusting God (sometimes without properly knowing him) to do the rest. The list is countless and as well as the household names like Oxfam, Christian Aid, Save the Children and so on includes personal friends of ours from the recent past, such as Hope for Justice, Christians against Poverty, Street Angels, Compassion, Stop the Traffik and Oasis.

Midge Ure reminded us of the value of small beginnings when he spoke at our ROC Showcase in Glasgow. His song, "Feed the World: Do They Know It's Christmas?" (which is the UK's second best-selling single of all time after "Candle in the Wind") featured a vast group of British and Irish musicians as part of the charity Band Aid. The initiative was launched in 1984 by Bob Geldof and Midge Ure to raise money for anti-poverty efforts in Ethiopia. They released the song for the Christmas market that year. The single surpassed the hopes of the producers to become the Christmas number one. Ure and Geldof's fundraising target was just £70,000, but it yielded a staggering £8m. The following year Live Aid went on to raise £150m.

SUPPLY AND DEMAND

Those of us involved in ROC have been on our own journey of faith, learning the lesson of the loaves, and it's far from being over. September 2014 is our tenth anniversary and our work has radically changed and grown since we first started. We are better placed now to meet a variety of social needs in more places than ever before, with a bigger staff team, more ambassadors, regional coordinators and volunteers. And yet the demand is always greater than our resource. We continue to punch way above our weight and each year we find ourselves expanding our response to the growing demand with nothing like the budget we need to deliver the goods. The lesson of the loaves. The need we see around us is always our motivation:

- 5,000,000 people aged 65+ say TV is their main companion
- 50% of adolescent crime is committed by children under 15
- 40% of unemployed people are under 25
- Suicide is the most common cause of death in men under 35

Rather than being intimidated by these statistics, they inspire us to respond at a greater level. Enquiries come in to our Manchester HQ daily from all over the UK and we try to keep pace with them as best we can. We've learned that the best way is to prioritise according to need and where we have good contacts in place.

I suppose it was only a matter of time before we decided

to go for Blackpool ROC! It just sounds like an idea waiting to happen, doesn't it? But it wasn't actually on our radar and we were too busy in other parts of the country to consider it. Then I read a headline in a paper which pushed me to do something: "Declining seaside towns in parts of the UK are stuck in a cycle of poverty, a think tank has warned". The story went on to explain that The Centre for Social Justice (CSJ) set up by Work and Pensions Secretary Iain Duncan Smith, had commissioned a report that said some towns were suffering "severe social breakdown". They were also becoming "dumping grounds" for vulnerable people such as children in care and ex-offenders. This has been "further depressing the desirability of such areas and so perpetuating the cycle," it said.

The CSJ report, entitled Turning the Tide, examined conditions in five coastal towns in England and Wales – Rhyl, Margate, Clacton-on-Sea, Blackpool and Great Yarmouth.

Whilst each town has its own particular problems, it said "a recurring theme had been that of poverty attracting poverty". A number of reasons were given including the idea that adults recalled happy childhood memories from seaside visits and this gave the towns a false, idealised image in people's minds; rents are cheaper making living costs lower; seasonal vacancies attract unskilled, unemployed applicants, but out of season there are fewer jobs.

Of all the towns listed in the report Blackpool is closest to our HQ and we had some good contacts there already with a couple of churches and senior police officers. I mentioned our interest to one or two people and doors began swinging widely open.

As usual, our first step was to organise a ROC Conversation event which took place in September 2013 in the Army Barracks.

The event was packed to the doors with a number of agencies present and a great turnout from Christians representing a number of local churches. The feedback was very positive and we are now planning a number of ROC projects which address social issues including anti-social behaviour, poor self-esteem, unemployment, low aspirations and repeat offending.

The support we have received from agencies across the board has been really encouraging. As well as some great churches we've got more groups than ever fully involved: the Fire and Rescue Service, Police, NHS, Council, One Blackpool, CVS and a number of smaller voluntary agencies. As a result of extensive consultative work we are about to set up a range of community based projects to meet a range of social needs in North, South and Central areas of Blackpool.

Again, we are on the very edge of our circle of comfort here, but putting our loaf-learning into practice. We'll offer our limited resources to the Lord and go for it, trusting him for things like more staff, buildings and, of course, the funds to pay for all the new projects.

PROVISION FOLLOWS VISION

One of the biggest lessons we've learned exactly mirrors the feeding miracle. When we look at the needs and the resources we need to address in setting up new projects, we consistently feel like those first disciples coming to Jesus with a handful of food and thousands of mouths. Rather than employing the traditional mind set of operating within our means, we step out in faith and start planning projects before we have enough people to run them or funding to finance them. God has never yet let us down and we have no reason to believe that he will.

We have experienced hundreds of these kinds of situations. The demand for ROC projects way exceeds our resource in terms of the staff we need, office space, finances, hours in the day. Our staff team has been way too small to achieve a national vision. It always amuses me when people ring our office and ask to be put through to various departments. I have a great team around me, but we all share the work at every level.

We have undertaken enormous steps of faith like organising massive city-wide and county-wide events costing huge amounts of money each time and the finance has always been provided. When you're sure you're doing what God has called you to do, there's every reason to believe that he will provide. When we sat down a few months ago to plan our recent launch in Glasgow we were a bit concerned to see the figures adding up to £40,000. At that point I did have second thoughts for a number of reasons: we only knew a handful of people in Scotland and the main person who had invited us a year ago was the Chief Constable of Strathclyde. In the last few months there had been wholesale changes in the policing infrastructure and now there was only one Police Force for the whole country, Police Scotland, with a different Chief who didn't know us at all. We had no contacts in the business community and no idea where to start fundraising for the event. Additionally, I had just learned that our status as a registered charity in England was not recognised north of the border. We would have to start the whole process of applying to the Office of the Scottish Charity Regulator. The good news was that we had five good Christian contacts and two friends in statutory agencies – enough raw material for a miracle. So we went for it. The short version is that we paid all the bills. I was hoping for baskets full of leftovers, but that wasn't to be!

THE LESSON OF THE LOAVES

Becoming aware of another major need in society prompted us, a year ago, to "step out of the boat" once more. I was on a train to London in the company of Greater Manchester Police Assistant Chief Constable Garry Shewan. Garry had kindly given up a day to visit our ROC mentoring scheme based at The Arc in Newham, London. On the train we got onto the subject of restorative justice which isn't surprising since he is the Association of Chief Police Officers national lead for this. My knowledge of restorative justice (RJ) was limited to say the least. I had heard something about victims of crime being encouraged to meet face to face with the perpetrators and, to be frank, the idea made me a little uncomfortable. Our house had been recently burgled and the last thing I would want to do if the burglar had been caught would be sit down and have a cup of tea with him.

Thankfully, Garry was able to set me straight on a number of misconceptions, including the idea that such a scenario would never be encouraged if the victim was unwilling. He is passionate about the subject and its many benefits both to victims of certain crimes and to those who commit them. Many young people who get into petty crime are vulnerable themselves to being drawn into a world that will shape their future very badly.

As an example, he told me about a conversation he'd had only the day before with a solicitor friend: a few months previously, a teenage boy had stolen his friend's bike and the mother reported the crime to the police. "That's how it started," the solicitor said, "but it soon spiralled into a sentence in a detention centre and later a prison sentence." The solicitor had said, "He's a nice lad really, I had a Christmas card from prison from him. But prison has become a way of life for him now." He finished by saying,

"I just wish this young man had gone through the RJ process in the beginning and maybe prison could have been avoided." Apparently, rather than the lad entering the Criminal Justice System and receiving a custodial sentence, the matter could have resolved by a Community Restorative Justice Panel, had one existed in the area. If the lad had been genuinely sorry and either been able to return the bike or pay back the value, then the Panel would have had the power to issue a caution with terms and conditions agreed to be appropriate by all parties.

Research has shown that RJ could save the UK £1billion over ten years if widely used and there is a strong and growing evidence base that it meets the needs of victims and reduces the frequency of re-offending. I have included some more information in the appendices but here are just a few examples:

- The majority of victims chose to participate in face-to-face meetings with the offender when offered by a trained facilitator.
- 85% of victims who took part were satisfied with the process.
- RJ reduced the frequency of re-offending, leading to a £9 saving for every £1 spent on restorative justice.
- 70,000 school age children enter the Criminal Justice System every year.
- Nearly half (42%) of all first time offenders are young adults.
- The number of 15-17 year olds in youth custody has more than doubled in the last 10 years.
- Two thirds of those imprisoned lose their jobs, a third lose their homes and 40% lose contact with their families.
- The reoffending rate amongst those aged 18-20 released from short term prison sentences (12 months or less) is 75%.

- Apart from the human cost, the amount of money spent in relation to dealing with young offenders is staggering. The total cost to the Criminal Justice System is estimated at approximately £4 billion per year.

Garry asked if RJ was something ROC could get involved in, considering our big community footprint and proven track record in meeting other social needs and our ability to raise up volunteers across many sectors. His vision is for community panels of trained volunteers who can help facilitate discussions not just between victims of certain crimes and those who have committed them, but also, for example, neighbours who are in dispute over, say, trees that are blocking light or dogs that bark at night – the kind of issues that can be prevented from escalating badly if they are addressed early enough; the sort of things that can enhance community life or damage it badly.

Victims of crime and anti-social behaviour can often feel disempowered by the Criminal Justice System. Often when they report an incident the matter is taken out of their sight and the solution administered is not always something that the victim wanted. Victims can benefit enormously from the chance to explain the impact of a crime and seek an apology from an offender. 85% of victims who have engaged in RJ conferences were satisfied with the experience.

Research into the use of RJ demonstrated significant reductions in the rate of reoffending for both young people and adults. We believe that the voluntary sector, and in particular churches, can make a significant contribution to RJ. As we know, churches have much to offer and many churches have a desire to engage more effectively with their communities, particularly with young people.

I found myself once more reflecting on the lesson of the loaves. We had neither the time nor the specific experience to even consider branching out to meet this need, but I knew that if we offered the little we had – in this case, just one well-placed advocate who believed in us and a reputation that could open some doors – then God would do the rest. I knew I would have a tough time persuading my team to take this on, so I did what I always do when faced with challenges like these – I talked to the Lord.

A few days later I happened to be speaking to a trust who liked our work but couldn't support our existing projects because of their specific remit. In fact, what they were looking to fund was community RJ initiatives! Thank you Lord.

Now don't get me wrong. I'm not saying you can turn your hand to anything. You need the right raw material for God to use. In this case we had the two things which were often missing in projects that were failing – the ability to raise up committed volunteers and the relationship with public services who have confidence in us and will therefore refer cases. The funder liked our proposal and we appointed a full time ROC Restore national development manager in February 2013. A year later we have dozens of volunteers trained, two more staff appointed to the ROC Restore team and three successful neighbourhood resolution panels in place, all in partnership with good strong churches who see this as a key way of blessing their community and building bridges for the Gospel.

THE NEXT CHAPTER FOR ROC

At the beginning of 2013 I wrote to all of the Police & Crime Commissioners across the UK to tell them of our work and request a meeting. To date I have had sixteen meetings which have opened up more opportunities and new project ideas. We have been asked to consider tackling: mental health issues, legal highs, repeat-offending, family mentoring, issues relating to early years and drug and alcohol addiction. When you rattle off lists like that doesn't it remind you of the work of the enemy? Jesus talked about the gates of Hell and how the Church would break them down. I am determined to take the fight to the enemy and see the Kingdom prevail. We can do this together as the Church. Redeeming communities means taking back what the enemy has stolen from people and turning whole neighbourhoods around for God. Surely these are just the issues we need to be addressing as part of our demonstration of the Gospel.

One of the Crime Commissioners spoke of a £1 million innovation fund which would support projects which are new ideas. I recognise in this the need for us to come up with creative, innovative things to address the pressing needs in our society today. This has prompted us to explore new ideas and new partnerships, such as new links with universities and colleges where we are collaborating around the idea of student placements, community research and even putting ROC projects into university campuses.

God has opened up new doors with influential people. In 2012 I received a letter from Buckingham Palace. To be honest I thought I might be in trouble for something! Too many speeding fines perhaps. But it was good news. I was being awarded an OBE in the Queen's birthday honours list. My first response was to burst into tears, mainly because my mum told me that she thought I would get an OBE a few years before she died. She spoke prophetically about my potential, which I couldn't see for myself. I was very touched that she believed in me and I was also very mindful of all of the great work being done by the unsung heroes in our projects, so I considered myself blessed to receive the honour.

In October 2013 our ROC team had a whole month of prayer to seek God for the next phase of the ROC journey. God spoke to us through many people and in many ways, including our friend James Aladiran from Prayerstorm who quoted from Joshua 3:5: "Consecrate yourselves, for tomorrow the LORD will do amazing things among you." New things were on the way. We are now on the brink of a greater step of faith.

A number of quite remarkable things happened during that month, one of which was that we were invited, out of the blue, to consider applying for the Community Asset Transfer of a large, multi-purpose community centre not far from our current HQ. At the time of writing I can't say too much about it as we're in the middle of a sensitive process of communication with various official bodies but, if everything goes through, it will be both the biggest breakthrough we've ever seen and, at the same time, the most faith-stretching venture we've ever been involved with. We'll move our HQ there and have a bit more space to function effectively. But, far more importantly, we'll be able to create a flagship of ROC projects on our own doorstep that will make a huge impact on the surrounding area (one of Greater Manchester's most deprived estates).

ROC has operated for ten years following the principles talked about in this book:

- Starting small.
- Having a glass half-full mind set.
- Trusting the Lord.

- Miraculous partnering with anyone who shares the vision, and...
- Stepping out in faith using the raw material we have, even when the opportunities appear to be off the scale compared with our resources.

It's been an amazing journey so far, but I'm more excited by the next ten years.

I love the line from the Chris Tomlin song that says, "For greater things are yet to come. And greater things are still to be done..."

I want to encourage you to step out in faith and see "impossible" things happen in your community. We would love to support and encourage you along the way.

Why don't you **ROC Your World**?

Vist the www.rocyourworld.org site

RECENT ENDORSEMENTS

"The ROC staff and volunteers are working hard to bring people together locally, but the impact is felt further afield too, and it's a testament to the real progress that is being made. It is vital that we create partnerships and work as a team to ensure that this real energy and commitment is turned into real long term, sustainable, results. I am determined to play my part in this."
Tony Hogg,
Police and Crime Commissioner of Devon and Cornwall.

"Working with ROC is part of our commitment to strengthen working with local communities. People of faith are often driven to make that faith come alive through reaching out to people in need in their area. Practical action like opening a youth facility, a lunch club for the lonely, a debt counselling service or mentoring scheme all help to create active communities where people work together and feel safer and less suspicious of each other as a result. Policing only succeeds through this sort of joint effort and individual officers have received great strength from the support they have been shown."

Sir Peter Fahy,
Chief Constable: Greater Manchester Police.

"I am delighted that Police Scotland is associated with Redeeming Our Communities. The organisation has a great track record of bringing churches, communities and organisations like the Police together to keep people safe and help find solutions all across the UK. Redeeming Our Communities' message is a simple one: 'together we are stronger.'"

Sir Stephen House,
Chief Constable: Police Scotland.

"The Scottish Fire and Rescue Service is delighted to be involved with Redeeming Our Communities. Their work has already proven to be very successful in bringing a range of partner organisations together to deliver positive outcomes for communities. The Fire and Rescue Service welcomes the chance to work closely with the organisation to enhance partnership working and improve the safety of our communities."

Peter Murray,
Assistant Chief Officer: Fire Scotland.

"I believe Redeeming Our Communities play such a valuable role in inspiring the Church to play its part in changing society and helping to connect churches with organisations and institutions that can help make them truly effective. The impact that ROC initiatives have on a local level reverberate on a national scale, delivering real change to the people who need it the most. CAP is delighted to be working so closely with ROC in serving communities across the UK."

Matt Barlow,
Chief Executive: Christians Against Poverty UK.

"I recently visited two ROC Centres and was deeply impressed with the level of motivation and commitment displayed by the staff, volunteers and supporters, all of whom are working extremely hard to improve the quality of life in their local communities by providing a wide range of opportunities for people. In doing so, they were obviously enjoying themselves and benefitting from the many friendships they have made."

George Almond CBE, DL,
High Sheriff of Greater Manchester.

"Supporting safer communities is a key tenet of the new Northern Ireland Community Safety Strategy, 'Building Safer, Shared and Confident Communities'. The newly established Policing and Community Safety Partnerships will be central to the delivery of this strategy. I was interested to hear of the work of ROC in various areas of Great Britain and believe ROC has a valuable contribution to make in Northern Ireland. I am keen to see the Department of Justice working with faith groups and local voluntary bodies to build positive partnerships and find practical solutions to local problems."

David Ford MLA,
Northern Ireland Minister of Justice

"Redeeming Our Communities offers an innovative approach in

galvanising our communities so that they are empowered and enabled to deal with a range of social problems including anti-social behaviour and recidivism. Devon and Cornwall Probation Trust fully supports this new initiative."

Simon Perkins,

Partnership and Joint Commissioning Manager: Devon and Cornwall Probation Trust.

"The remarkable short history of ROC has brought individuals and churches to a deeper understanding of how to impact their communities and how to develop creative partnerships to enable good things to happen. The respect and credibility that they have earned has opened doors into Government and brought about lasting change even in the toughest environments. The dedication and love that so many volunteers have demonstrated has brought hope and direction to many people and places that have lost sight of the God who loves them. I believe the energy and creativity that ROC offers can be a key agent of transformation for good in this country and beyond."

The Venerable Ian Bishop,

Archdeacon of Macclesfield

"Community agencies and people of faith share a passion to see people safe and thriving. ROC provides a framework for that shared passion to be turned into action. They act with integrity and commitment to be a transforming force for good in our communities and I am delighted that we have developed such a strong working relationship with them."

Peter Dartford,

Chief Fire Officer/CEO, Staffordshire Fire and Rescue Service

"Redeeming our Communities is a unique organisation with a full and practical track record of bringing Police, churches and communities together for the benefit of all. I have been hugely impressed, not only by the events that inspire and challenge, but by the initiatives, problem solving and friendships that have resulted. Across the UK people are coming together with their Police to make a real difference, bringing hope and transforming lives."

Matt Baggott,
Chief Constable: Police Service of Northern Ireland

APPENDIX I
2013/2014 ROC Café Feedback Report

(All names have been changed to protect the identity of the young people). 116 young people took part in a recent ROC Café feedback survey. Here are the results:

- 87% reported they have made new friends with young people.
- 70% reported that they made friends with volunteers.
- 44% reported that they have made friends with Police or Fire and Rescue officers.

When asked, has your opinion changed about Police and Fire Officers/volunteers?
62% reported that there had been a positive change in their opinion.

When asked why they attend the ROC Café:
- 71% reported that it is a safe and relaxed place to hang out with friends.
- 72% because it has lots to do like games, craft etc.
- 65% because it has as a tuck shop/food
- 48% because it offers workshops like beauty, cooking, sports, etc.
- 36% because it offers help with school work

When asked, have the things above helped to improve your confidence/self-esteem?

66% of all young people stated they felt their confidence/self-esteem had improved

When asked, have you learnt new skills? (e.g. in a workshop on the harmful consequences of crime, anti-social behaviour, fires, health and safety, first aid, tuck-shop skills, volunteering/work experience, baking, craft etc.)
61% stated that they had learnt new skills and explained what in most cases.

What the ROC Café Young People say:

Katy, 10, reported: "Now I don't swear and I tell my friends not to … I have learnt to control my anger."

Sarah, 12, said that her confidence and self-esteem had improved because, "I feel more confident to meet new people and make new friends."

John, 17, when asked whether his opinion had changed of the Police/Fire and Rescue said he was, "Not as scared of them now."

Rebecca, 12, said that her confidence and self-esteem had improved because, "I am very shy and me making friends has really boosted my confidence."

Amy, 16, reported that, "Nikki is a friend now and not just a Police Officer." She also said that her confidence had improved because, "I use to grunt at people and now I talk to them."

Billy, 13, said his confidence/self-esteem had improved: "I feel more relaxed and I feel like I can talk to more people. And I feel more safe because people are nice to me inside and outside the youth club premises."

Isabel, 16, said she, "has more confidence now, and not just hide behind my hoody."

Sabina, 16, said "Before the ROC Café my gang always got blamed for everything on the estate, but now through coming to ROC they (the Police and Fire and Rescue) treat us like human beings." She also reported that her self-esteem had improved and explained, "I use to self-harm. Since coming to ROC Café I don't any more."

Similarly, Erica, 13, reported that, "Mandie (the project leader) has taught me to love myself. I don't self-harm no more."

Gerry, 17, reported that her opinion of the Police has, "changed a great deal. Use to get in trouble a lot, but by being around officers at ROC I am now at college studying public services. I want to be a Police woman ... through gaining more confidence, I have so much more respect for people and myself."

Hinna, 11, reported, "I've learnt new skills in the tuck-shop – how to handle money and how to handle hot water."

Ed, 12, said his confidence/self-esteem has improved, "because [ROC Café] helps keep me calm while I'm with people ... because I have learnt how to cook and get along with people."

Isaac, 13, said his opinion hasn't changed because, "the Police will always protect you and stop criminals and the Fire Brigade also keep you safe and I guarantee you that the volunteers will look after you and make you feel safe."

Joe, 13, said he has learnt loads of new skills: "Baking, craft, the harmful consequences of crime, anti-social behaviour, fires, health and safety and volunteering responsibility."

Kirsty, 11, said that her opinion of the Police/Fire and Rescue had changed because, "I thought they were nasty, but now I know I can trust them and they care about us all."

APPENDIX II

From The Restorative Justice Council

RJ Works - The Evidence

The Government funded a £7 million, 7-year research programme looking into restorative justice. In her independent evaluation, published in four reports (see "Ministry of Justice Evaluation" below) Professor Joanna Shapland found that in randomised control trials of RJ with serious offences (robbery, burglary and violent offences) by adult offenders:

- The majority of victims chose to participate in face-to-face meetings with the offender, when offered by a trained facilitator
- 85% of victims who took part were satisfied with the process
- RJ reduced the frequency of re-offending, leading to £9 savings for every £1 spent on restorative justice

Expert independent criminologists Professor Lawrence Sherman and Dr Heather Strang state that the reduction in the frequency of re-offending found in this research was 27% – that's 27% less crime, 27% fewer victims following RJ.

Alongside the Sentencing Green Paper in December 2010 the Government published their own further analysis of the data behind the Shapland reports, quantifying the size of the reduction in the frequency of re-offending following RJ as 14%.

This strong evidence of an impact on re-offending is backed up by evidence from Northern Ireland where Youth Conferencing forms the main approach to all youth crime; and by international research evidence (see further reading below).

Cost-benefits

Working from the data in Professor Shapland's reports, the Restorative Justice Council and Victim Support presented the Government with evidence that providing restorative justice in 70,000 cases involving adult offenders would deliver £185 million in cashable cost savings to the Criminal Justice System over two years, through reductions in re-offending alone.

The Matrix Report – an independent expert analysis of the economic benefits of restorative justice – has revealed that restorative justice would likely lead to a net benefit of over £1billion over ten years. The report concludes that diverting young offenders from community orders to a pre-court restorative justice conferencing scheme would produce a life time saving to society of almost £275 million (£7,050 per offender). The cost of implementing the scheme would be paid back in the first year and during the course of two parliaments (10 years) society would benefit by over £1billion.

Restorative Practice in Schools

There is good evidence that restorative practice delivers a wide range of benefits for school communities. Recent independent evaualtions of restorative practice in schools have shown that:

- Whole-school restorative approaches were given the highest rating of effectiveness at preventing bullying by a report published by the Department for Education, with a survey of schools showing 97% rated restorative aproaches as effective.
- In Barnet, an evaluation by the local authority found a reduction in exclusions of 51% in RJ trained schools; compared to a 65% increase in exclusions in the thirty two

Barnet schools that have received no RJ training. They also found increased confidence among school staff to deal with bullying and conflicts in the school.

- An independent evaluation of Restorative Justice in Bristol schools found that restorative justice improved school attendance and reduced exclusion rates.
- In Hull, a two-year Restorative Justice pilot led to 73% fewer classroom exclusions, 81% fewer fixed term exclusion days, a reduction in verbal abuse between pupils and verbal abuse towards staff of over 70%.

(Source:www.restorativejustice.org.uk/restorative_justice_works/)

APPENDIX III
Neighbours from Hell?

A local housing association referred a neighbour dispute case to ROC Restore as it was becoming a nightmare for their staff to deal with. One of the neighbours was calling them on a weekly basis to complain about his female neighbour and demanding his neighbour be evicted. In his opinion, he had more rights since he owned his own home and she was a tenant whose rent was being funded by the housing association. He complained that his neighbour played her music too loudly and often in the early hours of the morning. He said his daughter, aged 6, was being affected by the loud music played at unreasonable hours. He shared custody of his daughter with her mother and only had her to stay a couple of nights each week. Due to the noise she was saying to her mother that she didn't want to stay at her Daddy's house any more. The housing association issued letters to their tenant threatening her with warnings of eviction and saying that they were going to fit noise monitoring equipment in her neighbour's home to build their case for eviction. However, when noise monitoring equipment was fitted there was no noise detected – which they assumed was because she had been warned and so was making sure she was quiet until they removed the equipment.

ROC Restore volunteer facilitators went to visit both parties involved to find out what was going on. They met with the lady to get her side of the story. She painted a very different picture indeed. She said that the man next door made too much noise doing DIY very late at night and that they should ask other neighbours on their row of houses who would confirm this. She went on to explain that they were previously in a relationship and used to spend a lot of time together. They fell out a couple of years ago and didn't speak for some time. Then he started putting his rubbish in her bin and in her garden. He was also using her back garden as a cut through and he had moved one of the fence panels to the side so he could do this. She also suspected that he may have tapped into her electricity and gas supplies, as he was an electrician and her bills had gone up significantly.

When they visited the gentleman who was complaining he explained that this had been going on for 2 years and that he finally decided to make a formal complaint 6 months ago. The noise monitoring equipment had been fitted 5 times and each time she would just stop making noise while the equipment was in and start again when it was removed. As the equipment was very expensive the housing association refused to leave it in his home. He expressed how angry he was that she would get a letter informing her of the date when the equipment would be fitted and for how long, so she had warning. The facilitators did notice that he was in the middle of doing up his house, so they asked him about the work he was doing and he talked them through how he had completely renovated his property and was nearly finished.

The volunteers then went to neighbouring houses to ask if those residents had experienced any noise from either of the properties in question. All the neighbours confirmed that both houses contributed to noise on their street.

The volunteers asked each party if they would like to bring a supporter to the subsequent conference to discuss their problems. The man declined, but the lady wished to bring her mother. The mother relayed how upsetting this had been for the whole family and how worried she was that her daughter may get evicted. She didn't believe that her daughter was playing loud music and said that the man was making it up.

It became clear that both the parties involved were at fault in some way and that it was a case of tit for tat. Both parties agreed to take part in the face-to-face conference and a date was agreed. The day before the conference the man cancelled due to work commitments so the volunteers needed to rearrange. When the date arrived the lady called to cancel as she was not feeling well. The volunteers sensed that she may be trying to get back at him, but persevered and rescheduled. They thought it would be prudent to meet with each party individually again to ensure the conference ran smoothly and nothing unexpected would happen.

The day of the conference came, for a third time. The volunteers asked the lady with her mother to arrive first as they felt she was the most vulnerable. She was very nervous and said that she nearly changed her mind, but she turned up because of the hard work of the volunteers and she didn't want to let them down.

When her neighbour arrived the room was very tense indeed. The way that we seat parties in a circle, facing each other, means that they are forced to look at one another, which can create tension but is vital in enabling clear communication. As the process began the volunteers stressed the ground rules of respecting one another and allowing each person to talk without interruption, as everyone would get their turn to speak.

The restorative questions are the essence of any restorative approach and form the basis of the concise script which the volunteers use. The questions are open and flexible and can be used with offenders, victims and supporters in addressing behaviour in restorative conferences or with individuals in the preparation phase of the process:

- What happened?
- What were you thinking at the time?
- What were you feeling?
- Who has been affected?
- What needs to happen now?
- What do you need to do now?

As each party answered the questions everyone in the circle began to relax. Each party accepted their part in this dispute and both apologised to the other. The lady agreed not to play loud music between 10pm and 8am and to be mindful at weekends when the man's daughter was staying. He agreed to pre-warn her should he be carrying out any building work. Both agreed to speak to each other and be civil, solving problems as and when they may arise in a reasonable manner. Both parties left together and continued to talk outside the conference venue.

Satisfaction surveys are completed for both parties 1 month after the conference: she stated that things have been "really good – I went into the process not expecting much. However, now I have had the meeting I feel much better. My neighbour and I are on civil terms and I even took a parcel in for him. No further incidents since the meeting." He said, "I appreciate all the hard work of the volunteers and am really pleased with the outcome we agreed."

The volunteers thoroughly enjoyed the whole experience and said it was miraculous to see how the restorative justice process brought about reparation and unity between the people involved. It really does repair the harm caused and build a kinder community to live in.

CONNECT WITH ROC UK

Email: info@roc.uk.com

@debrajgreen
@ROCUK2014
@ROCreativemedia
@rocyourworld1

www.facebook.com/redeemingourcommunities

Main website: www.roc.uk.com
Book website: www.rocyourworld.org